DAVID GILLICK'S

KITCHEN

DAVID GILLICK'S KITCHEN

Good food from the track to the table

MERCIER PRESS

IRISH PUBLISHER – IRISH STORY

MERCIER PRESS
Cork
www.mercierpress.ie

© David Gillick, 2015

Photographed by Rob Kerkvliet – A Fox In The Kitchen
Styled by Orla Neligan of Cornershop Productions
www.cornershopproductions.com
Assisted by Joanne Arnold and Vanessa Stanley

Image p. 23 © INPHO/Getty Images; p. 79 © Pat
Murphy/SPORTSFILE; p. 82 © Tomas Greally/SPORTS-
FILE; p. 94 © Brendan Moran/SPORTSFILE

Book design (interior) by Fidelma Slattery

PROPS SUPPLIED BY

Avoca: HQ Kilmacanogue, Bray, Co Wicklow.
(01) 2746939; info@avoca.ie;
www.avoca.ie

Meadows & Byrne: Dublin, Cork, Galway, Clare,
Tipperary. (01) 2804554/(021) 4344100;
info@meadowsandbyrne.ie;
www.meadowsandbyrne.com

Marks & Spencer: Unit 1–28, Dundrum Town
Centre, Dublin 16. (01) 2991300;
www.marksandspencer.ie

Article Dublin: Powerscourt Townhouse, South
William Street, Dublin 2. (01) 6799268;
items@articledublin.com;
www.articledublin.com

Dunnes Stores: 46–50 South Great Georges
Street, Dublin 2. 1890 253185;
www.dunnesstores.com

Harold's Bazaar: 208 Harold's Cross Road,
Dublin 6W. 0877228789.

Historic Interiors: Oberstown, Lusk, Co Dublin.
(01) 8437174; killian@historicinteriors.net

TK Maxx: The Park, Carrickmines, Dublin 18.
(01) 2074798; www.tkmaxx.ie

Bakers Bling on Etsy:
www.etsy.com/shop/BakersBlingShop

Fired Earth: 19 Great Lower Georges Street,
Co. Dublin. (01) 6636160;
www.firedearth.com

A. Rubanesque: (01) 6729243;
ribbons@arubanesque.ie; www.arubanesque.ie

Tiger Stores: (01) 598 8800; www.tiger-stores.ie

Optica: 1 Royal Hibernian Way, Dublin 2.
(01) 6774705; www.optica.ie

ISBN: 978 1 78117 382 4

10 9 8 7 6 5 4 3 2 1

A CIP record for this title is available from the
British Library

This book is typeset in True North Regular,
and Frutiger.

Printed and bound in the EU.

**THERE ARE SO MANY PEOPLE I WOULD LIKE TO THANK
THAT IT'S HARD TO KNOW WHERE TO START.**

My wife **CHARLOTTE** has been a massive source of inspiration, advice and support. She has been there throughout all my highs and lows and I couldn't have written this book without her.

To my parents, **JIM** and **SHEILA**, and my family, I don't say it enough, but thank you for everything you have done for me.

To Charlotte's parents, **KEITH** and **AUDREY**, and to all the Wickhams, who have been a constant support to me since day one.

To **SARAH LIDDY** and **THE TEAM AT MERCIER**, this book simply would never have happened if you didn't believe in me.

One of toughest weeks I have ever had was spent in the kitchen photographing the dishes for this book, but the skilled partnership of **ORLA NELIGAN** and **ROB KERKVLIET** made it fun and full of laughter.

To **SONIA** and **CATHY HARRIS**, thank you for making this book a reality.

Over the years I have crossed paths with so many inspirational people who have made me a better person. I can't thank you all enough. To **JIM KIDD** and the **COACHES AT DUNDRUM SOUTH DUBLIN ATHLETIC CLUB**. To **NICK DAKIN**, my long-term coach, you brought me to a level I only dreamed of as a kid. **ENDA MCNULTY**, you challenged me and made me believe and realise my potential. I owe you so much.

The inspiration to get into the kitchen came from **MARTIN MACDONALD**, an incredibly talented nutritionist who I had the pleasure of working with to become the best I could be.

To **MY TRAINING GROUP** in Loughborough, the band of brothers I shared so much with over the years, thank you for pushing me on a daily basis and forcing me to raise the bar.

CONTENTS

DINNER

DESSERTS

INTRODUCTION

> ## 'A GOAL WITHOUT A PLAN
> ## IS JUST A WISH.'
>
> ANTOINE DE SAINT-EXUPÉRY

Food wasn't something I gave much thought to when I was growing up. I was the youngest of four kids – three boys and one girl – and to say dinnertimes were busy is an understatement. Meals were always homemade and we seldom ate out. I can even remember the weekly routine. Monday was mince and potatoes, Tuesday was lamb chops, Wednesday was ham, Thursday was stew, Friday was pizza and chips, on Saturday you had to fend for yourself and Sunday was a roast.

My mum was a nurse and worked the night shift, so she would get up after working through the night at around 4 p.m. By then I would be home from school, so my jobs included peeling the spuds, bringing the ham to the boil and turning on the oven. I didn't know it at the time, but looking back, our home-made meals had an effect on me and it's something I carried through to my athletics career.

EARLY YEARS

Athletics has always been a part of my life, and indeed my family's life. The Ballinteer Community School, home of the Dundrum South Dublin athletics club (DSD), was at the end of our road. Every Tuesday and Thursday my parents would ship us all down to the running club for a few hours.

This is where it all started. I was always the fastest on my street and in my classroom, but I never imagined athletics would become my career. I fancied myself as a premier league footballer!

I played a variety of sports growing up, including football, GAA and, of course, running. I had success on the track in my early years, winning the Dublin interschools each year for my national school, Our Lady's Boys Ballinteer. At that point I was also doing well for my club, DSD. I enjoyed athletics and the other sports I was participating in, but something started to change in my mid-teenage years. I started to lose. Kids I used to beat hands down began beating me and I wasn't winning medals at local track and field competitions. The teenage years are a funny time. Kids become adolescents at different rates and this obviously has an impact in sport. Looking back, I was a late developer and this may be why I started to lose a few races. It was frustrating to lose races that I used to win, but I kept at it. I'm not really sure why – maybe deep

down I knew things would come good – but it's fair to say I did enjoy the training, even though competitions weren't going my way.

My secondary school, St Benildus College in Kilmacud, had a proud tradition of cross-country running and we were a competitive team. We won plenty of Leinster medals and an All-Ireland bronze, which I think had an influence on keeping me in the sport. I was part of a winning team, and it's always nice to get on the podium!

I had a breakthrough in fifth year at St Benildus. I matured and as a result found my niche event in athletics. For the first time in my young running career, I won an individual All-Ireland schools gold medal for the 400 metre hurdles. I couldn't hurdle well, but my speed and strength carried me through. At that moment, I realised I had a talent.

TURNING POINT

I gave up football and concentrated on GAA and athletics, as I felt I was better at those sports and was making more inroads. I continued with both until the end of 2002. That summer I was chasing the qualifying standard for the IAAF World Junior Championships in Jamaica. The standard was 48.0 seconds; I ran 48.48 and missed the qualifying time. Thankfully, Athletics Ireland had sent a 4 x 400 metre relay team, which I was picked for. The experience was unreal. I vividly remember standing in a packed stadium along with 40,000 others watching a young Usain Bolt tear up the track, the whole stadium shouting, 'Bolt! Bolt!' The seed was planted. I wanted more of this.

I decided to give up GAA and concentrate solely on athletics. That was it – one sport along with studying full time. I wanted to run fast. I wanted to represent my country at the major events, including the Olympics.

I trained hard, and in 2005 I won my first major medal as European Indoor 400m Champion. Things happened fast that year. I had never run a full indoor season, but as it progressed, my times were decreasing and I was moving up the rankings. When the championships came around, I was in the hunt.

That winning weekend in 2005 propelled me into full-time athletics. I finished my degree in 2006 and I remember talking with my parents in the sitting-room, Mum doing the ironing, Dad reading the paper, about what I was going to do next. I wanted to run full time, but I knew I needed to take it to the next level. I had a great coach in Jim Kidd here in Dublin and I was confident in his ability, but I wanted more. I wanted to be in a full-time environment with athletes who were faster than me, which would force me to raise my game.

I made a promise to myself. I didn't want to turn thirty and look back and say, 'I

wonder what would have happened if I had given running a real go.'

I decided to move to Loughborough in England to further my athletics career. Up to then I had been living at home, studying for a degree and trying to fit in training six times a week around everything else. I was busy and I often let certain aspects of my game slip. I remember being so frustrated as I lay in bed at night, thinking that I should have done better, I should have eaten a better lunch, I should be resting more, I should have given myself more time. I would look at other international 400-metre athletes and wonder what made them so great. Were they eating a ham salad roll for lunch?

I never really had anyone give me advice on nutrition, on goals, on building a support team or on making a plan to achieve my potential. I realised then that I had a shelf-life and that it was time to take ownership of my talent and my plan.

While training in the gym one day, I crossed paths with Enda McNulty, the former Armagh All-Ireland GAA footballer and sports psychologist. Enda helped me with my decision to move to the UK and put the wheels in motion. He also challenged me about how I was going to reach my long-term goal of representing Ireland in the 2008 Olympics.

Up to that point, I had thought that writing a goal on a piece of paper and sticking it on my bedroom wall was enough. Enda asked me a simple question: 'What is your goal?' I said I wanted to run faster than 45.5. Why 45.5? Because in 2006 that was the Olympic and World Championship qualifying standard. No Irishman had run faster than 45.58. Enda then asked, 'Well, how are you going to achieve that?' I had never really thought about what I needed to do or how I was going to do it. I had simply thought that I just needed to train harder.

THE FOUR PILLARS

My goal became clear. I knew what I wanted to achieve. I started to work backwards and look at the areas I needed to improve on. These areas included MINDSET: goals, plans, building confidence and dealing with nerves; EXERCISE: my training and finding areas where I needed to improve, not just on the track or in the gym, but getting stronger and improving my speed over shorter distances; NUTRITION: eating the right foods, fuelling my body correctly and recovering optimally (did I need to gain weight or lose weight?); and finally, REST AND RECOVERY: was I recovering after training and getting enough sleep at night? Was I trying to do too much outside athletics and was it affecting my training, my life? These are the four pillars of peak performance and I needed to take ownership of them.

I built my plan as a pyramid, with my goal at the top and all the blocks that were going to help me achieve it underneath.

BACK TO BASICS

Living away from home for the first time, I had to learn some basic life lessons, such as how to use a washing machine, make a bed, iron a shirt and how to cook. Up to that point my mum had cooked a lot of what I ate. She is a good cook and, as I said earlier, a lot of what we ate was real, home-cooked food.

I had learned the basics from Mum, but now I was keen to bring it to another level. I started to read more about food and sports nutrition and I went to a few seminars. I learned a lot, but there weren't a lot of practical tips, such as what food to eat, how to cook and how to make food taste nice.

Just before I moved to Loughborough I was at home having breakfast with my dad. I had porridge with a scoop of protein powder. I may as well have taken a bite out of the kitchen table – it was dry and horrible. I added a teaspoon of olive oil and almost got sick. I remember thinking, 'This had better be worth it!' My dad looked on as he enjoyed a nice boiled egg on toast.

I knew the benefits of good nutrition, but it wasn't until I decided to spend a bit of money and go to a nutritionist that I noticed a real change.

Being surrounded by world-class athletes in Loughborough illustrated the importance of having a good support team. The

THE FOUR PILLARS
OF PEAK PERFORMANCE

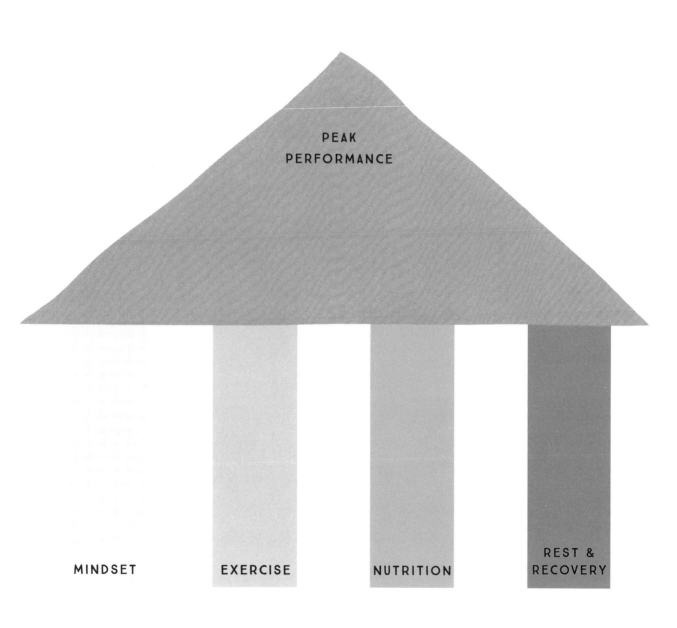

PEAK
PERFORMANCE

MINDSET   EXERCISE   NUTRITION   REST & RECOVERY

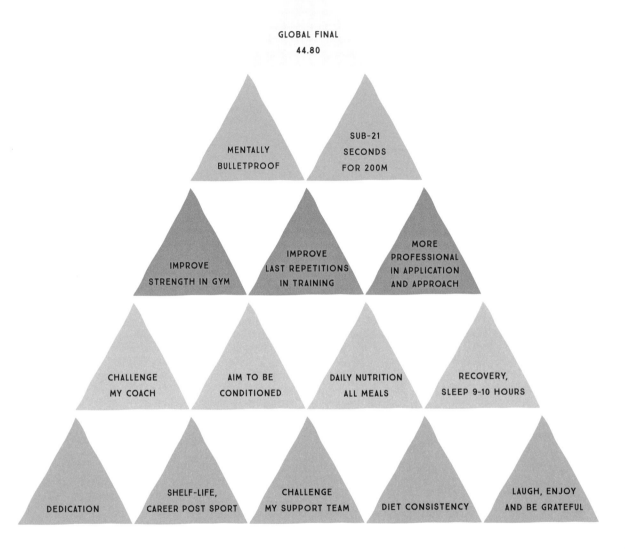

GLOBAL FINAL
44.80

MENTALLY BULLETPROOF

SUB-21 SECONDS FOR 200M

IMPROVE STRENGTH IN GYM

IMPROVE LAST REPETITIONS IN TRAINING

MORE PROFESSIONAL IN APPLICATION AND APPROACH

CHALLENGE MY COACH

AIM TO BE CONDITIONED

DAILY NUTRITION ALL MEALS

RECOVERY, SLEEP 9-10 HOURS

DEDICATION

SHELF-LIFE, CAREER POST SPORT

CHALLENGE MY SUPPORT TEAM

DIET CONSISTENCY

LAUGH, ENJOY AND BE GRATEFUL

THE GOAL PYRAMID

athletes I was training with had a back-up team of doctors, physios, nutritionists, strength and conditioning coaches and even psychologists. I said to myself, 'I want some of this.'

So I built my own team – Team Gillick. A key member of this team was my nutritionist, Martin MacDonald. I learned a phenomenal amount about food from Martin. Martin's approach was all about real, unprocessed food. He focused on my daily diet and how it could help to fuel, repair, recover and prepare my body for training and competition, as well as prevent injury. The first question Martin asked me was what I enjoyed eating and what foods I liked. It wasn't about bigger muscles, buying big tubs of powder or changing everything about how I ate overnight.

Not only did we work on my daily diet, but he also made sure I was correctly fuelled for my most important races and that my body could fight off infections and any stress-related illnesses. Food became my medicine.

A NEW PASSION IS BORN

This ignited something within. I loved talking about food, and when I learned about what was in food and how to cook it, mainly by trial and error, I enjoyed it. Cooking became therapeutic. It actually helped me switch off from thinking about my training or upcoming races. I found I

was watching a lot more cooking shows, including *MasterChef*, and I would try to replicate certain dishes by adding in alternative ingredients to make them a little healthier.

Training six times a week takes its toll on the body and the mind. Stress and tiredness can leave your body open to a whole array of illnesses, so it is vitally important to make sure you are doing everything you can to keep you on track – a lesson that's also true in everyday life.

I began to look at the ingredients in food when I shopped. I would spend hours in the supermarket, walking around and learning more about the food on offer. I started to understand much more about the roles protein, carbohydrates, fat and fruit and vegetables play in the body. As a sportsperson, your health is your wealth and I decided I was going to leave no stone unturned in my preparation to become a world-class athlete.

You might think I was eating huge amounts of calories during training, but you'd be wrong! As a 400m athlete, the focus isn't on size, but rather, recovery. I was eating roughly 2,500 calories a day, which is the recommended amount for an average adult male.

I focused on timings and eating consistent, real food throughout the day. It wasn't rocket science, but eating the right food became as important as my training on the track.

I do believe I was talented, but at this level all athletes have talent, and some more than me. But I worked hard and made sure that I was a true professional and looked after everything. I wanted to stand on the track behind the starting blocks and look at my competitors and know that I had given 100% to my preparation. It gave me confidence.

Nutrition became a key pillar of my performance, along with mindset, exercise and recovery. I built it into my routine and it became part of my life.

It doesn't matter whether or not you exercise – you can still reap the rewards of a good diet. Losing weight, toning up or just taking better care of yourself can all lead to better self-esteem, more confidence, more energy, increased productivity, a better appearance and, above all, happiness.

TOP OF MY GAME

The following four years were my best. I retained my European Indoor title in 2007 when I won the 400m in a new Irish record of 45.52, which was also inside the Beijing Olympics qualifying time of 45.55. I had just won my second major title and booked my place for the Olympics. It was a good day.

I improved my outdoor time to 45.25 that summer and also made the semi-finals of the World Championship in Osaka. I improved again in 2008, when my per-

sonal best sat at 45.18. I was getting close to that 45-second barrier, but the 2008 Olympics didn't go well. I came down with a virus in the holding camp prior to travelling to Beijing and I ran poorly in the competition. I was devastated.

After the Olympics experience, I asked myself some tough questions and came to the conclusion that I had simply forgotten to enjoy my sport. I had got caught up in the Olympics buzz for the entire year. I tried to do everything to 110% and never allowed myself to switch off. I got very anal about what I was eating and would even worry that if I ate 50g more sweet potato it would affect my performance.

The result? I stressed myself out.

I promised myself that in 2009 I would work hard but would press the off button now and again and enjoy the fact that I was doing sport as a career. If I fancied eating a pizza or having a beer with mates, I would.

The mindset worked and 2009 was my best year. My time improved and I loved every minute of it. I ran 44.77 and came sixth in the Berlin World Championships. It was a dream come true. I always wanted to make a global sprint final and consistently run against the best 400m athletes in the world. 2009 was a massive step forward for Irish sprinting and I would like to believe it gave confidence to other Irish sprinters that we can sprint and challenge the best of them.

I was consistent in 2010, again running under 45 seconds regularly. I made the final of the 2010 World Indoor Championships and also finished fifth in the European Championships. But I was disappointed not to win, and I had to take stock again. I decided to move to America. There were still two years to go until the London Olympics and I felt I needed to improve my speed in order to progress and win medals. The training group I joined in the USA had some of the fastest athletes on the planet.

TIME TO HANG UP MY SPIKES

My time in the States didn't work out and in 2011 I returned home badly injured. I initially tore my soleus muscle in my calf, followed by Achilles problems. I made two consecutive attempts to come back after the soleus injury of 2011, one in 2012 and then again in 2013. After the disappointment of not making the London Olympics in 2012 due to injury, I decided to give it another go in a new environment down in Australia. Unfortunately, injury struck again and after twelve years of training for one of the hardest events in athletics, I decided to hang up my spikes.

Retirement is hard. It takes a long time to adjust to the massive change in routine. Not training to the same intensity or degree as a full-time elite athlete is another frustration.

At first I didn't want to have anything to do with athletics. I stopped training and didn't care about what I was eating. I felt horrible, not only physically but also mentally. I soon realised that eating well and training regularly were my drugs. I needed them in my life.

CELEBRITY MASTERCHEF IRELAND

I was training in Canberra, Australia in 2013 when I got an email about taking part in *Celebrity MasterChef Ireland*. The email arrived two days after I tore my Achilles tendon in training. I was down in the dumps and wasn't sure if I was ever going to run again. I wasn't in a good place. I jumped at the opportunity; I love all the *MasterChef* shows and have watched them all over the world.

About two days later, though, my thoughts were a lot different from my initial reaction. 'What have I let myself in for?' I thought. 'I can't cook! I only know one way to cook and I cook the same meal over and over!'

Prior to the show, the producers asked if it was possible for me to get into a working kitchen to see how it all works. The last time I had been in a working kitchen was when I was fifteen years old, working as the dishwasher in my local Chinese restaurant in Dundrum. The washing machine had broken and apparently I was the man for the job. I got paid three punts an hour and always came home with free chicken balls and chips. Somehow I didn't think chicken balls and chips would go down well with either Nick Munier or Dylan McGrath, the two judges on the show.

Near the house in Canberra was a restaurant that the locals had told me had a good reputation, so I took the plunge and asked if they could help me out. I explained what I was undertaking and they showed me the ropes. I spent one week dropping in for a few hours here and there, and the kitchen staff were great. I learned an awful lot simply by watching them. They encouraged me to help out too, chopping, cooking and of course sampling the menu! The big thing I took away from the kitchen was how to cook meat and fish properly and what goes well with certain foods, such as avocado with halibut.

I also took note of the menu and learned what changes I could make to a dish to make it a little bit more balanced, like using quinoa as a crust instead of breadcrumbs or serving mashed sweet potatoes instead of champ.

By the end of the week, I was helping the kitchen out during service to paying customers. As a thank you they let me invite Charlotte and my housemate Alex to the restaurant for me to cook and serve what they ordered. When the food arrived they didn't believe I'd cooked it!

It was Alex who gave me the belief and confidence I needed. I was in the kitchen in the house practising some dishes and having a wobble about why I had agreed to do this whole thing in the first place when Alex simply said, 'You'll be surprised how much you actually know.'

He was right – I *was* surprised!

The first task of the show was called 'You on a Plate'. We were asked to create a dish that illustrated our backgrounds and personality. I decided to make a salmon fillet with asparagus salad and tabbouleh (see page 128). We had 90 minutes to do the task. This was when it got serious. One of the producers started the stopwatch and away we went. I didn't realise that the timing was going to be so strict. If they said you had 90 minutes for a task, you had 90 minutes. If the dish wasn't ready, tough.

The process was hard, and the fact that the two judges, Nick and Dylan, were wandering around the kitchen, standing over your shoulder watching what you were doing but saying absolutely nothing, made you question your actions. It reminded me of a school test, with the teacher looking over your shoulder and making you wonder if you had answered correctly.

It was nerve-racking and I was constantly guessing what the next task could be. It was like studying for an exam when you don't even know the subject. The crew never let anything slip. We would be at them the whole time trying to get a clue as to what they might have planned next.

At the same time, the buzz was brilliant. You would be told to wait outside the kitchen and then, when shouted at, you would start the walk in, heart pounding, dreading what was coming next. Nick and Dylan would give the orders and the stopwatch would start. We were off and all hell would break loose in the kitchen. We were like headless chickens running around trying to grab ingredients before someone else did and then trying to think of how to cook them.

Each task was very different and took me out of my comfort zone. As the competition went on, the judges got a little stricter, bringing the real kitchen attitude to the fore in not tolerating mistakes, dirtiness or delays.

As each task passed and I remained in the kitchen, I began to enjoy it. I was still nervous about what I was doing and thought, 'I'll be found out soon', but I loved the nerves, as it reminded me of the anxiety that builds up before a race. You sit around waiting to enter the kitchen, similar to the call room before going onto the track in a stadium, and then boom, the gun goes off and you have to perform – only this time it was cooking. The post-task euphoria was great. You're relaxed, glad the task is over and that you've got through to the next round, just like post-race excitement. I enjoyed the buzz, and the more tasks I got through, the more I wanted to stay in.

Things wobbled in the semi-final, when we were down to the final four. The task was to cook whatever we wanted from the pantry. Being allowed to pick whatever we wanted sounds great, but that was the difficult part. There was so much choice – what do I put with what, what should I mix and match, what if I do too little or too much? I decided to keep things simple and went with scallops cooked in mint butter served with a crispy pancetta salad.

It sounds straightforward, but I panicked. I left the scallops to last and I lost control. I didn't want to cook them too early, but when the producer started shouting that we only had 20 minutes left, I lost it and burned them to a crisp. They were like ice hockey pucks. I barely had enough time to get another batch cooked and onto the plate. I had the producer, Nick and Dylan all shouting at me to hurry up. I think they were loving the fact that I was crumbling before their eyes.

'Stop what you are doing! Time over!'

I looked at my plate and then looked at Aengus Mac Grianna's, Maia Dunphy's and Yvonne Keating's and thought, 'I'll get my coat.' I honestly thought I was going home. My dish looked terrible compared to theirs.

As always, they made us wait for the decision. I was livid with myself about messing up a simple dish. 'I'll never cook scallops again!' I fumed.

Eventually we were brought back into the kitchen and told the verdict. I was

nervous, convinced I was going home. Fortunately, they kept me in and sent Yvonne home. I think the fact that I didn't serve the burnt scallops and cooked another batch went in my favour. They did say my presentation was shocking but that the dish tasted good.

I was delighted to make the final. I hadn't dreamt for one minute I would get that far, and after the semi-final I thought, 'I'll just enjoy it now. I haven't disgraced myself, thank God!'

The final was a different story. The task was to cook a three-course meal, starter, main and dessert, within three hours. I could plan for this, so I stuck to what I knew. I would start with quinoa-encrusted lamb cutlets, followed by pan-fried halibut on a bed of avocado and celeriac re-moulade, finished off with a summer meringue torte.

The final took place in Dubai, so it was brand new surroundings. I had got used to the *MasterChef* kitchen. I knew where everything was and how to use the equip-ment. Now I couldn't even find a fork in the place.

Three hours may sound like a long time, but it isn't. The time flew by and it was important to have a plan, which thank-fully I did. I started with the dessert first, as it takes a bit of time to make the meringue. I then moved on to the re-moulade, which requires making mayonnaise, which is tricky.

The kitchen wasn't the biggest, so we were all running around each other and all the camera and crew. It was stressful. One big factor this time was that I could clearly see what Aengus and Maia were making. That's the funny thing about *MasterChef*. Nobody makes the same dish so it's hard to compare, but at this stage of the competition you think, 'Is that dish better than mine? Are they showing more skill?' To be honest, I felt I was the under-dog in the final. Aengus and Maia knew what they were doing, but I thought that if I could make my dishes well with no mistakes, then I had as good a chance as they did.

I was first to present, and after three long hours in the kitchen, including having to redo both my mayonnaise and crème Chantilly, I got my dishes to Nick and Dylan. They both take a bite and say nothing. Sit back, chew a little and look at each other. Dylan goes back for more – surely that must be a good sign? Moving on to the main, they try a little, then try a little more. Say nothing. Finally, dessert. They still don't say anything.

At last, they speak. They're impressed. They like my dishes. They're not big fans of having lamb cutlets for a starter, but they say it was nice nonetheless. They like my main and my dessert is lovely.

I was delighted, relieved, shattered and drained, but thrilled. I had tried to do it well with no mistakes and I had achieved that. I couldn't have done any more.

Maia was next. At that point I was back in the waiting room and didn't know what was going on. When Maia came back to the waiting room, she wasn't happy. She'd messed up her dessert and said the feedback from the judges could have been better. Aengus was out next, and similar to Maia, something had gone wrong and the judges noticed. It was at this point that I started to think I might be in with a chance of winning! My feedback had been good. I suddenly got a bout of nerves.

The next few hours dragged. Nick and Dylan went off to deliberate and we sat outside in the heat, glad it was all over but also nervous about what was to come.

Finally, we were whisked off to the pool area. The stage was set with all the lighting and cameras. The producers had us standing exactly where they wanted us, in a row, side by side. I started overanalysing. 'Why are we standing in this stance? Does it mean something? Just get on with it!' Nick started to speak but kept messing up his line. Take one, take two. Eventually he spat out his lines and over to Dylan, back to Nick. They were having a laugh here.

After what seemed like an eternity, they announced me as the winner. I was shocked and speechless. I had never thought I could win something to do with cooking! The champagne was popped. I felt overwhelmed by what had just happened. As the show wasn't going to air until August and it was only early June, I had to keep quiet about the entire experience, never mind the fact that I had won. At that time I was also moving back home to Dublin and was back in my small bedroom in Ballinteer in Mum and Dad's house temporarily. I couldn't say a word, so I had to smuggle in the trophy and bury it in the back of the wardrobe for the next three months.

On my return from Dubai my parents asked me how it had gone. 'I'm not going to ruin the show for you,' I said. 'You'll just have to watch it.' They guessed I had made it to the final simply because I had gone to Dubai and because the fast taxi had been coming to the door for the last three weeks to pick me up.

The whole experience was amazing. I never thought I would win. To be honest, it was one of the hardest things I have ever done. The long days coupled with not knowing what the tasks were made it physically, mentally and emotionally exhausting.

When I won, it gave me a massive lift at a time when I was extremely low and thought I was just an athlete and was only good at one thing: running. It put a smile on my face and gave me a little bit of my swagger back after all the injuries and hardships my athletics career had thrown up.

THIS BOOK

The idea for this book came after my success on *Celebrity MasterChef Ireland*, which illustrated my approach to food. On the show I stuck to what I know: healthy eating. I have always been into food from a performance point of view, but also for general well-being.

Over the years, the top two questions I would be asked were how long I run for and what I eat. People were always surprised when I said I only ran for 400m, which only takes 45 seconds. As for food, most people think I must eat like a horse and are surprised when I say that as a sprinter, my calorie intake isn't too far off the standard recommendation of 2,500 calories a day.

The nutrition world is a minefield. One week we're told to eat a certain diet, but the next week it's something else. Diet nowadays sounds like a restriction and a timeframe. It gets too confusing and people just don't know what to eat.

I have tried most diets, including gluten-free and paleo. They all have their merits, but personally I feel that a balance works well as long as the main focus is on real, unprocessed food. I had my best years when I put this philosophy into practice and I still stick to it.

Keeping food simple and straightforward is sustainable and easier to maintain in the long run. This book aims to give you an insight into my approach to food, some tips on building a balanced dish and of course some of my favourite dishes.

• NOTE: ALL OVEN TEMPERATURES GIVEN IN THIS BOOK ARE FOR CONVENTIONAL OVENS. FOR FAN-ASSISTED OVENS, SET THE TEMPERATURE 20°C LOWER THAN THE TEMPERATURE CALLED FOR IN THE RECIPE.

'YOU HAVE A TICKET TO THE BALL, NOW GO AND DANCE'

JIM KIDD [MY FIRST COACH]

Today, I try my best to stay in shape and it starts with being an elite in the kitchen. I'm passionate about real food, and, regardless of the exercise we do, it is vital that we eat more healthy, unprocessed foods.

I try to eat well most of the time, but it's important to be social and I enjoy eating out with friends and family. Too many rules and regulations will drive you mad. You also need to be able to switch off and find a good work–life balance. I learned years ago that if it puts a smile on your face, it can't be too bad … within reason!

Healthy eating is something everyone can do. All you need is willpower. Even after retiring from full-time training, I still try to keep things simple and stick to the key principles opposite. I don't get caught up on fad diets, which seem to change from week to week.

I like to treat myself now and again, so I generally try to abide by the 90:10 rule: I eat well 90% of the time and allow myself to have a treat 10% of the time.

KEY PRINCIPLES OF HEALTHY EATING

1.

EAT REAL FOOD

Stay away from processed food. If it swam, ran, flew or grew, eat it.

2.

DON'T SKIP MEALS

Try not to go long periods without eating.

3.

VARY YOUR INTAKE OF FOOD.

Don't just stick to the same foods – try to regularly vary what you're eating.

4.

THE MORE COLOUR, THE BETTER.

When it comes to fruit and veg, eat a variety of colour: a rainbow plate.

5.

BE WARY OF SO-CALLED 'LOW-FAT' PRODUCTS.

Generally they are over-processed and contain lots of sugar, preservatives and additives.

6.

STAY AWAY FROM SUGAR.

Aim to eat low-sugar food instead. This will help keep your insulin levels stable, which in turn will help keep hunger under control and keep your energy levels more constant too.

7.

INCLUDE GOOD FATS.

Good fats such as nuts, seeds, olives, feta cheese and avocados are staples in my diet. Always aim to include a source of good fat in your meal.

8.

REWARD YOURSELF WITH A TREAT OCCASIONALLY.

Stick to a routine and don't be afraid to reward yourself with your favourite treat. It's very common for people to have a treat meal once a week, so enjoy it and then get back on the wagon.

BUILDING A BALANCED DISH

Over the years, one of the key lessons I learned from nutritionists was how to build a healthy, balanced meal. It sounds so simple, but it's only when you take a good look at what you're actually eating that you realise that sometimes you're only eating one type of food.

Take breakfast, for example. How many people have toast and jam to start the day? There's only one food type here: carbohydrate. No protein, no good fat and no vegetables or fruit. While you sleep you fast, so the first meal of the day is important, and it's vital that it's balanced. Try to include a source of protein, vegetables or fruit and, if need be, a source of slow-release carbohydrate. I say 'if need be' because if you are trying to lose weight, you don't need to fuel up with carbohydrates. I'm not anti-carbs, but I think people are eating too many processed, poor-quality carbohydrates.

To explain how carbohydrates work in the body, let's use water as an example. Imagine I'm holding a glass of water that's three-quarters full in my right hand and a jug of water in my left hand. If I pour the water from the jug into the glass and continue to do so, it will overflow. But if I fill the glass to the top and then stop and take a drink from the glass, I can top up the glass with water from the jug. This is exactly how the body works, but with one big difference: when the water, i.e. the carbohydrate, overflows, it gets turned into fat and the result is weight gain. When we exercise, it's as though we're taking a drink from the glass and then we can refuel with a carbohydrate meal post-exercise. And the more we exercise, the more carbohydrate we can consume.

Your meals should contain sources from all the food groups. The more variety of foods and the more colour on your plate, the better.

To control portion size, use your hands. The palm of your hand should equate to the amount of protein that's on your plate, a fist for vegetables, half a cupped hand for carbohydrate and the length of your thumb for fat.

A BALANCED PLATE

The illustration opposite shows how I would build my plate on a day I exercised. If I didn't do any exercise I would reduce the amount of carbohydrate and increase the amount of vegetables.

RECOVERY SNACKS

* ★ BANANA

* ★ ORANGE JUICE

* ★ HANDFUL OF NUTS

* ★ WHEY PROTEIN

* ★ FLAVOURED MILK

* ★ FRUIT YOGURT

* ★ HEALTH BARS

Post-exercise, it's extremely important to refuel with a carb and protein snack in the 20 minutes immediately after training. The need for this is governed by how hard you have worked, i.e. the rate of perceived exertion. Or to put it more simply, the talk test. If you're doing a training session where the intensity is such that you can maintain a conversation, then you don't need a big recovery snack. If it's so intense that you can barely stand, never mind talk, then a recovery snack is required.

This is the only time that fast-release sugar is allowed, so it's okay to eat sugary health bars at this point.

SOME OF MY FAVOURITE FOODS

PROTEIN
Chicken, turkey, beef, eggs, tofu, fish and beans.

CARBOHYDRATES
Oats, sweet potatoes, quinoa, bulgur wheat, butternut squash and couscous.

FRUIT
I try to eat light-skinned fruit, such as blueberries, blackberries, raspberries, strawberries and plums, because they have more antioxidants and less fructose.

VEGETABLES
The more colour you can eat, the better. I tend to eat more above-ground veg, such as broccoli, courgettes and cauliflower, because they are lower in starch and don't affect insulin levels. Eating too much sugar and starch, which are present in root veg, can result in weight gain.

FAT
Rapeseed oil, olive oil, coconut oil, avocados, nuts, seeds, feta cheese, olives and mozzarella.

A MEAL PLAN FOR A TYPICAL WEEK

Retirement is hard. It meant a massive change in routine and, of course, not training to the same intensity or degree as a full-time elite athlete. So how do I stay in shape? It starts with being an elite in the kitchen. Below is a typical week for me in terms of what I eat.

BREAKFAST Bircher muesli (page 42)

SNACK Sliced apple covered in peanut butter

LUNCH Vegetable omelette

SNACK Olives and mixed nuts

DINNER Thai red chicken curry (page 145)

SNACK Greek yogurt, berries and chocolate (page 77) and peppermint tea

BREAKFAST Muesli (page 41) and Greek yogurt

SNACK Cottage cheese, fruit and cashew nuts

LUNCH Red lentil, chickpea and chilli soup (page 98)

SNACK Protein balls (page 70)

DINNER Mum's stew (page 163)

SNACK Yogurt mousse (page 78) and peppermint tea

BREAKFAST Breakfast smoothie (page 51)

SNACK Hummus (page 63) and sliced carrots

LUNCH Quiche (page 120)

SNACK Mixed nuts

DINNER Quinoa with salmon, rocket and mint pesto (page 156)

SNACK Red pepper and Boursin snack (page 67) and peppermint tea

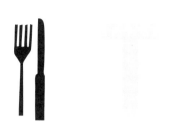

BREAKFAST Granola (page 45)

SNACK Cottage cheese, fruit and cashew nuts

LUNCH Thai chicken cups (page 114)

SNACK Protein balls (page 70)

DINNER Spanish omelette (page 119)

SNACK Greek yogurt, berries and chocolate (page 77) and peppermint tea

BREAKFAST Simple fast oats (page 46)

SNACK Mozzarella and tomato

LUNCH Chicken, quinoa and mango salad (page 113)

SNACK Greek yogurt and dessicated coconut

DINNER Mexican loaded potato skins (page 172)

SNACK Hummus (page 63) with celery sticks and peppermint tea

BREAKFAST Peanut butter cup smoothie (page 54)

SNACK Cottage cheese, fruit and cashew nuts

LUNCH Chicken and spinach wrap (page 104)

SNACK Protein balls (page 70)

DINNER Treat meal

SNACK Too stuffed! Peppermint tea

BREAKFAST Bacon and eggs with salsa (page 38)

SNACK Sliced apple and almond butter

LUNCH Mixed bean salad (page 117)

SNACK Mixed nuts

DINNER Roast dinner

SNACK Dessert and peppermint tea

BREAKFAST

> ## 'GIVE ME SIX HOURS TO CHOP DOWN A TREE AND I WILL SPEND THE FIRST FOUR SHARPENING THE AXE.'
>
> ABRAHAM LINCOLN

I have always loved breakfast and have never found it hard to eat a meal first thing in the morning. Some say it's the most important meal of the day, and I would agree. It's so important to start the day with a substantial, well-balanced meal. When I was training full time, breakfast was my biggest meal. I would aim to have it around two hours before I started training. It would keep me fuelled all through training.

My lifestyle today has changed somewhat since my training days, but breakfast is still important. If I'm not training I reduce my carbohydrate intake, but I still include good sources of protein, fat and vegetables or fruit.

It doesn't take long to prepare a good breakfast, and now that smoothies and juices are so popular, it's even easier to get all the goodness in at breakneck speed.

The danger of skipping breakfast is that you will end up snacking on sugary foods throughout the day and will never feel satisfied. It can even affect your performance over the course of the day.

TIPS FOR BREAKFAST

1.

Don't skip breakfast.

2.

Aim for balance.

3.

Ditch the high-sugar juices or dilute them with water.

4.

Stay away from high-sugar cereals.

5.

Eat more berries and add vegetables where you can.

6.

Eat slow-release carbohydrates, such as porridge.

7.

Always include a good source of protein, such as eggs, bacon, nuts, seeds or nut butter.

TWO-INGREDIENT PANCAKES

INGREDIENTS

2 eggs, lightly beaten
1 large banana, mashed
pinch of baking powder
pinch of ground cinnamon
1 tsp coconut oil or rapeseed oil

**MAKES 10
SMALL PANCAKES**

This is a really simple recipe, ideal for a quick, healthy breakfast before heading out to training or to the office. It's got everything you need to get going in the morning and you can top the pancakes with whatever you fancy – within reason, anyway!

Heat a 23cm pan over a medium heat.

While the pan is heating up, make the batter by mixing together the eggs, banana, baking powder and cinnamon in a bowl.

When the pan is hot, add the oil and let it heat through. Pour in 2 tablespoons of batter at a time and cook for 30–60 seconds, until the bottom appears to be set. Flip with a spatula and cook for an additional minute or less.

Serve warm and top with yogurt, berries and a pinch of ground cinnamon.

OAT PANCAKES

Eating the same breakfast every day can get a bit boring. One morning while eating my bowl of simple fast oats (page 46), I thought, 'What would happen if I put the contents of my bowl in a frying pan?' After a bit of tinkering, I came up with this take on pancakes.

Place the oats in a medium bowl and pour in just enough water to cover the oats. Microwave for 40 seconds.

Crack the egg into the oats and add a scoop of whey protein if desired. Mix really well with a fork.

Melt the coconut oil in a 23cm pan over a medium heat. Pour the oat mixture into the pan and fry for 3–4 minutes, until the bottom is light brown and cooked enough to be able to flip it over. Flip the pancake and cook for about 5 minutes more, until golden brown. An easier option is to place the pan under the grill to cook the top – leave the flipping to the pros!

Transfer to a plate and top with the Greek yogurt, berries and chopped nuts.

INGREDIENTS

60g porridge oats
1 egg
25g whey protein (optional)
1 tsp coconut oil
70g Greek yogurt
50g fresh berries
1 tbsp chopped nuts

SERVES 1

ALL-IN-ONE BREAKFAST

This is a great sharing breakfast that I picked up in Australia. The Aussies love a good brunch and I tried something similar to this in a café in Canberra. I'm a big fan of chorizo, so I have used it here instead of bacon and I've added kidney beans. With loads of flavour from the balsamic vinegar and Worcestershire sauce, it's a great dish to kick-start your weekend.

Preheat the grill.

Heat a large frying pan over a medium heat and add the diced chorizo. Cook for 2 minutes, until it has started to release its oil, then add the chopped tomatoes, green pepper, Worcestershire sauce and balsamic vinegar and season with salt and pepper.

Turn up the heat and leave for 4 minutes to let it reduce, stirring occasionally. Add the drained kidney beans and mix well.

Make four wells in the mixture and crack one egg into each well. Leave for another couple of minutes, until the bottom of the eggs turn white. Transfer to the grill and cook for another couple of minutes, until the eggs are cooked through.

Bring the pan straight to the table and let everyone help themselves.

BACON AND EGG MUFFINS

With Charlotte being from Sunderland in the UK, we are always having visitors staying over at our house in Dublin. Breakfast is a busy time, so I make it a little easier by cooking everything in the oven.

These muffins are great when cooking for a crowd. Some muffin trays can hold up to 18 muffins, so there is plenty to go around.

Preheat the oven to 180°C/350°F/gas mark 4. Grease six holes of a muffin tray with a little olive oil.

Melt the coconut oil in a large pan over a medium heat. Lightly fry the garlic and spinach until the spinach wilts.

If using rashers, slice them in half lengthways. Wrap the bacon around the edges of each muffin cup. Add some crushed garlic and wilted spinach. Finally, crack an egg into each hole with a pinch of salt and pepper.

Bake in the oven for 10 minutes, until the eggs are set. Serve with some toasted sourdough bread.

INGREDIENTS

olive oil, for greasing
1 tsp coconut oil
3 garlic cloves, crushed
handful of fresh spinach
3 rashers or 6 pieces of streaky bacon
6 eggs
salt and pepper

MAKES 6 MUFFINS

SMASHED AVOCADO ON TOAST

INGREDIENTS

½ ripe avocado
30g feta
salt and pepper
1 tsp lemon juice
1 slice bacon
1 tsp coconut oil
1 egg
1 slice of wholegrain bread,
toasted

SERVES 1

Who doesn't love eggs on toast? When I lived in Australia, my housemate Alex ate avos, as they call them, like they were going out of fashion. Always ripe and fresh, they were delicious and easy to use. I've added some feta cheese, which tastes great with the warm egg.

Mash the avocado and feta together in a bowl with a fork. Add some salt and pepper along with the lemon juice.

Cook the bacon under a hot grill until crisp, turning it every few minutes so it cooks evenly.

Melt the coconut oil in a small pan over a medium heat and fry the egg to your liking.

Spread the toasted bread with the mashed avocado. Top with the cooked bacon, followed by the fried egg.

BACON AND EGGS WITH SALSA

I eat a lot of bacon and eggs, which are a great source of protein and are very versatile. Grilled bacon is best, as it allows the excess fat to drip away. I'm always looking for healthy accompaniments to go with eggs and bacon, so this is my take on *huevos rancheros*.

Cook the bacon under a hot grill until it's crisp, turning it every few minutes so it cooks evenly.

Melt 1 teaspoon of the coconut oil in a medium frying pan on a high heat. Fry your eggs to your liking. When the eggs are ready, transfer them to a plate and keep them warm in the bottom of the grill.

Wipe out the frying pan and add the remaining teaspoon of coconut oil. Set the pan over a medium heat and add the chopped tomatoes, beans, peppers, celery, chilli and coriander. Stir continuously for 7–10 minutes, until the peppers are soft.

Add the tomato mixture to the warm plate with the eggs and add the bacon alongside. Garnish with a few leaves of fresh coriander. Serve hot.

INGREDIENTS

2 rashers
2 tsp coconut oil
2 medium eggs
100g tinned chopped tomatoes
100g tinned mixed beans
70g red and yellow peppers, chopped
50g celery, chopped
½ fresh red chilli, deseeded and finely diced (or a whole one if you like it hot!)
fresh coriander, chopped, plus extra to garnish

SERVES 1

MUESLI

INGREDIENTS

200g porridge or jumbo oats

50g almonds, chopped or flaked

50g walnuts, chopped

50g pumpkin seeds

50g hemp seeds

50g sunflower seeds

50g raisins or any dried berries
you like

50g desiccated coconut

50g dried apricots, chopped

50g dried figs, chopped

1 tbsp ground cinnamon

1 tsp vanilla extract

pinch of nutmeg

pinch of sea salt

SERVES 4-6

Not that long ago I was buying a box of muesli, and me being me, I looked at the ingredients. The amount of added sugar was alarming, so I put the box down and said I'll do it myself. My recipe is child's play: just throw everything in a bowl and enjoy with milk or yogurt.

This couldn't be easier. Simply combine all the ingredients in a large mixing bowl and stir until everything is evenly distributed. Store in an airtight container for up to one month.

Serve with milk, almond milk, coconut milk or Greek yogurt.

BIRCHER MUESLI

I first came across Bircher muesli when training in Australia. I would open the fridge in the morning and find a bowl of porridge ready to go. I tried some but it was a bit too sweet for me because the oats had been soaking overnight in apple juice. I decided to give it a go and changed the juice to non-dairy milk. You can add in your favourite berries and seeds.

Mix all the ingredients together in a large bowl. Cover with cling film and refrigerate overnight.

In the morning, transfer the Bircher muesli to individual bowls and top with fresh fruit, crunchy nuts or any other superfood you have on hand. My favourites are berries, sliced bananas and a dollop of yogurt.

INGREDIENTS

200g oats
500ml unsweetened coconut, almond or soya milk
3 tbsp currants
2 tbsp chia seeds
2 tbsp hemp seeds or milled linseed
2 tbsp coconut flakes or desiccated coconut
1 tbsp pumpkin seeds
squeeze of fresh lemon juice

SERVES 4

GRANOLA

200g organic rolled oats
50g puffed quinoa, rice or millet
40g stevia
1 tsp ground cinnamon
1 tsp sea salt
3 tbsp coconut oil
handful of unsweetened
desiccated coconut or
coconut shavings
handful of flaked almonds
handful of nuts, roughly chopped
(I recommend cashews and
walnuts)
handful of pumpkin seeds
handful of sesame seeds
handful of linseeds
handful of dried cranberries
and/or dried blueberries, goji
berries, etc.

SERVES 6

I love granola – anything crunchy always seems to find a way into my kitchen. As with muesli, I got frustrated with the amount of added sugars and syrups in shop-bought granola. To help cut out the sugar and still get the ingredients to bind together, I use coconut oil. I also use stevia to add a touch of sweetness without the side effects of sugar. Stevia is a natural sweetener that has zero calories, zero GI and is tooth friendly too.

Make a big batch of granola and have it ready for a quick breakfast at home, in the car or at the office. I've listed the ingredients I use, but you can use whatever berries, nuts and seeds you fancy.

Preheat the oven to 150°C/300°F/gas mark 2. Line a large baking sheet with parchment paper.

Combine the oats, puffed quinoa, stevia, cinnamon and sea salt in a large bowl.

Melt the coconut oil in a small pot set over a medium heat, then pour it over the oats mixture and mix well. Spread the granola on the lined baking sheet in a single even layer. Bake in the oven for 30 minutes, stirring every 10 minutes to keep it from burning.

After 30 minutes, add the coconut, nuts and seeds (if you add them earlier, they will burn). Bake for an additional 10–15 minutes. When your granola sounds crispy it's done. Remove from the oven and add the dried berries. Let it rest for about 15 minutes but do not stir. While resting, the granola will have a chance to stick together and clump up. When the granola is completely cool, store it in an airtight container for up to one week or in a ziplock bag in the freezer if it won't be used within a week.

Enjoy with Greek yogurt and fresh fruit.

SIMPLE
FAST OATS

This is my staple breakfast that I have been eating religiously for years. It takes a total of 3 minutes to make and you can't get a more balanced meal. Packed with long-lasting energy to keep you fuelled throughout the morning, some might say it's the breakfast of champions!

Place the porridge oats in a serving bowl and pour in enough water to just cover the oats. Cook in the microwave for 1 minute.

Remove from the microwave and stir in the berries, whey protein (if using), Greek yogurt, milled seeds and coconut oil (if solid, it will melt in the warm porridge). Mix well and sprinkle with a pinch of cinnamon. Serve straight away.

50g porridge oats
100g mixed berries (frozen are fine – just place them in a separate cup and microwave for 1 minute)
30g vanilla-flavoured whey protein or your favourite flavour (optional)
2 tbsp Greek yogurt
1 tbsp milled seeds or chopped nuts
1 tsp coconut oil
pinch of ground cinnamon

SERVES 1

GREEK YOGURT AND BERRIES

INGREDIENTS

130g Greek yogurt
70g frozen or fresh berries
30g vanilla-flavoured whey
protein or your favourite
flavour (optional)
2 tbsp chopped nuts
1 tbsp honey

SERVES 1

I love Greek yogurt. High in protein, low in carbs and sugar free, it's great with muesli and granola but it's also a brilliant snack between meals, in the office or out on the road.

———————————————

Place the Greek yogurt in a bowl and mix in the berries, whey protein (if using) and chopped nuts. If using frozen berries, thaw them in the microwave for 1 minute before adding to the bowl. Finish with a drizzle of honey.

GILLY'S OAT BREAD

Bread can be a difficult thing to substitute, so I'm always on the lookout for great-tasting alternatives. I won't lie – I'm more of a cook than a baker, but even so I had fun putting this recipe together.

Oat flour is just finely milled oats. You can buy it as flour or make it yourself by whizzing oats in a food processor.

Preheat the oven to 180°C/350°F/gas mark 4. Grease a 2lb loaf tin.

Mix together the oats, oat flour, mixed seeds, baking soda and salt in a large bowl. In a separate bowl, mix together the Greek yogurt and mashed banana. Add to the dry ingredients, mixing well to combine.

Scrape the mixture into the greased loaf tin and bake for 40 minutes (check it at 35 minutes). The bread is done when the top springs back lightly when you press it with your finger and it sounds hollow when tapped under-neath, or if a tester (a toothpick or knife) inserted into the centre comes out clean, with no raw batter clinging to it.

INGREDIENTS

1 tsp butter or solid coconut oil,
for greasing
150g porridge oats
150g oat flour
6 tbsp mixed seeds, such as
pumpkin, flax, sesame
1 tsp baking soda
½ tsp table salt
500g Greek yogurt
1 banana, mashed

MAKES 1 LOAF

BREAKFAST SMOOTHIE

INGREDIENTS

50g porridge oats
30g whey protein (optional)
1 banana
100ml orange juice (not from concentrate)
100ml water
2 tbsp Greek yogurt
1 tbsp chopped nuts
1 tbsp seeds
3–4 ice cubes
2 tbsp Udo's Choice ultimate oil blend

SERVES 1

I started drinking smoothies when my coach decided to change our training times to early mornings. Breakfast is extremely important and I couldn't do without it, so in order to get it into my body faster, I throw all the ingredients into a blender and boom, 30 seconds later I have a liquid breakfast.

You can put whatever you like in a smoothie – it's trial and error! Optional extras or replacements include any good-quality nut butters, frozen or fresh berries, any fruits, avocados, kale or spinach. I also add 2 tablespoons of Udo's Choice oil to my smoothie to boost my intake of good fats. Good fats in the form of omega 3, 6 and 9 fatty acids from coconut and flax, sunflower and sesame seeds are great for overall health and well-being. They help improve skin, hair and heart health, keep joints supple, boost energy and aid recovery from exercise. Udo's Choice is a staple in my diet as it tastes great and is very versatile.

This couldn't be easier. Simply place all the ingredients in a blender and whizz until smooth. A hand blender will also work – just put all the ingredients in a jug and blend.

GREEK YOGURT AND BERRY SMOOTHIE

I'm a big fan of Greek yogurt and it has become a staple in my diet. By itself the yogurt can be bland, so adding a few different real berries and blending it really brings it to life.

If using frozen berries, there's no need for the crushed ice.

Place all the ingredients in a blender and whizz until smooth. If it's very thick you may need to add a drop of water to help it blend.

INGREDIENTS

200g Greek yogurt
100g blueberries
100g raspberries
100g strawberries
1 banana
1 tbsp ground cinnamon
crushed ice (optional –
see introductory note)

SERVES 1

PEANUT BUTTER CUP SMOOTHIE

Avocado in a smoothie? I know, I thought the same, but to my surprise it went down very well. This recipe will fill you up and is a great way of getting healthy fats and proteins into your diet.

Halve the avocado and scoop out a quarter of the flesh and place in a blender. Add the remaining ingredients and whizz until smooth.

INGREDIENTS

¼ ripe avocado
1 tbsp peanut butter
25g chocolate-flavoured whey protein
10g cocoa powder
200ml milk
pinch of sea salt

SERVES 1

STRAWBERRY AND ALMOND SMOOTHIE

4 ice cubes
100g fresh or frozen strawberries
200ml chilled almond or soya milk
2 tbsp almond butter

SERVES 1

A great snack to have at home or bring with you on the go. Only three main ingredients makes it very quick and easy to make.

––

Place all the ingredients in a blender and blend until smooth.

SNACKS

'THE PLANE ALWAYS TAKES OFF INTO THE WIND.'

IN CONVERSATION WITH PADRAIG O'CEIDIGH

What we eat between meals is just as important as the main meal itself. Snacking keeps energy levels consistent throughout the day, yet snacks are where we fall down, grabbing the easy ready-made high-sugar biscuit, yogurt or piece of chocolate that keeps calling your name.

For example, take a normal lunchtime meal at 1 p.m. followed by dinner at 6 p.m. – that's five hours with nothing in between. The result is low energy and tiredness, which affects your performance in the late afternoon. The best way to combat this is by snacking on good-quality, low-sugar foods.

I always aim to eat every two or three hours. This includes having a good snack between my lunch and dinner at around 4:30 p.m. – the afternoon slump.

WHEN PUSHED FOR TIME, MY READY-MADE SNACKS INCLUDE:

★ MOZZARELLA CHEESE AND SLICED TOMATO

★ A HANDFUL OF MIXED NUTS

★ OLIVES AND MOZZARELLA

★ QUARTERED APPLES WITH PEANUT BUTTER

★ GREEK YOGURT AND CRUSHED NUTS

★ NATURAL YOGURT AND DESICCATED COCONUT

★ COTTAGE CHEESE, FRUIT AND CASHEW NUTS

★ A SMALL SALAD WITH A GOOD SOURCE OF PROTEIN

★ GREEN TEA

★ FRUIT

★ NUTS

★ DRIED MEAT (JERKY)

I know that not everyone has access to the above foods all the time. Even if you end up in a shop or filling station, many of them are beginning to provide better-quality products. You just need to spend some time looking around the shop to find them.

AVOCADO AND GREEK YOGURT DIP

Healthy homemade dips are a great way to snack throughout the day. Having one or two dips in your fridge is a great stand-by when the afternoon slump hits so that you can reach for some healthy veg instead of a sugary biscuit. Dips go great with toasted bread, carrot batons, celery sticks and rice crackers as well as Mexican dishes and salads.

Scoop the avocado flesh into a bowl and mash with a fork. Stir in the yogurt, coriander and lime juice and transfer to a serving bowl.

1 ripe avocado
150g Greek yogurt
1 tbsp chopped fresh coriander
1 tsp lime juice

SERVES 4

HUMMUS

200g tinned chickpeas
2 garlic cloves, crushed
3 tbsp Greek yogurt
2 tbsp lemon juice
2 tbsp tahini
1 tsp ground cumin
1 tsp paprika

SERVES 4

Drain and rinse the tinned chickpeas, but keep the liquid. Combine 4 tablespoons of the reserved liquid with all the other ingredients in a food processor. Blend to a creamy purée. Add a little more lemon juice, cumin or paprika if desired.

Store in an airtight container in the fridge and consume within four days.

BABS' GUACAMOLE

Babs is a friend of mine who made this the night the final of *MasterChef* aired. We ate far too much of it and now guacamole always reminds me of that evening.

Scoop the avocado flesh into a bowl and mash with a fork. Stir in the diced tomato, half the chilli and the diced onion along with a good squeeze of lime juice. Mix well and add a pinch of salt and pepper. Taste the guacamole and add more chilli or lime juice, depending on your taste buds.

Store in an airtight tub and consume within two days.

INGREDIENTS

2 ripe avocados
1 ripe medium tomato, diced
1 fresh green chilli, diced
½–1 red onion, diced
juice of 1 lime
salt and pepper

SERVES 6

SALSA

Place all the ingredients in a bowl and mix well. Cover with cling film and place in the fridge for a few hours to let all the flavours blend together. Serve chilled.

500g ripe tomatoes, chopped
70g onion, finely diced
2 garlic cloves, crushed
1 small jalapeño, seeded and finely chopped
2 tbsp fresh parsley, chopped
2 tbsp lime juice
pinch of salt

SERVES 4

RED PEPPER AND BOURSIN SNACK

INGREDIENTS

½ red pepper
50g Boursin cheese

SERVES 1

Simply cut the halved pepper into thirds and then load up the hollow of each pepper slice with the cheese. It's quick and easy to make and tastes lovely!

Keep chilled if you're not eating these immediately.

KALE CRISPS

INGREDIENTS

bunch of fresh kale
1 tbsp olive oil
1 tsp sea salt

SERVES 2

Preheat the oven to 180°C/350°F/gas mark 4. Line a baking tray with parchment paper.

Using a sharp knife, carefully remove the leaves from the thick stems. Discard the stems and tear the leaves into bite-sized pieces.

Wash and thoroughly dry the kale with a salad spinner. Drizzle the kale with the olive oil and sprinkle with the sea salt.

Bake for 10–15 minutes, until the edges are brown but not burnt. Eat straight away.

PROTEIN BALLS

Mix all the ingredients together in a bowl until well combined. Divide into eight equal portions and roll into balls
between the palms of your hands.

Sprinkle some extra coconut in a shallow bowl and roll
the balls in it. Chill until ready to eat. Store in an airtight
container in the fridge for up to five days.

INGREDIENTS

50g porridge oats
30g shredded desiccated coconut,
plus extra for coating
10g chocolate or vanilla-flavoured
whey protein
4 tbsp good-quality low-sugar
peanut butter
2 tbsp honey
1 tbsp cocoa powder

MAKES 8 BALLS

CHOCOLATE CHIP COOKIE DOUGH PROTEIN BARS

INGREDIENTS

4 scoops vanilla-flavoured
whey protein
6 tbsp coconut flour,
plus more if required
4 tbsp good-quality low-sugar
peanut butter
130ml almond milk,
plus more if required
1 tsp ground cinnamon
125g 80% dark chocolate

MAKES 6 BARS

Does a chocolate chip cookie dough that's good for you sound too good to be true? Then you will be pleasantly surprised when you try these bars.

Line a 2lb loaf tin with cling film.

Put the whey protein, coconut flour, peanut butter and almond milk into a large bowl and mix until combined. If the mixture feels very dry, add a tiny bit more milk. If it feels too wet, add a tiny bit more flour – but only a little at a time. The mixture needs to be soft and squishy, but not so soft that the bars won't hold their shape. Once you've reached the right texture, add the cinnamon.

Take half of the dark chocolate and break it up into very small chunks. Stir the pieces of dark chocolate carefully into your mixture, trying to distribute them evenly through the dough. Transfer the dough to the lined loaf tin.

Melt the remaining dark chocolate by placing it in a heat-proof bowl set over a pot of gently boiling water. Using a spoon, drizzle the melted chocolate over the dough in the tin.

Transfer the tin to the freezer for 3–4 hours to allow the chocolate to harden and set. When it's frozen solid, remove the tin from the freezer. Using the cling film, lift the dough out of the tin and cut the solid block into six bars. Wrap each bar in cling film.

Store the bars in the freezer. When you feel like a snack, take one out and let it thaw for a few minutes.

GILLYBARS

These are my homemade version of a flapjack. They're ideal as a snack, at home or out and about. You can put in any of your favourite dried fruits or nuts.

Preheat the oven to 180°C/350°F/gas mark 4. Line a deep baking tray with parchment paper.

Mix all the ingredients together in a large bowl. Use your hands and make sure all the ingredients are well combined.

Transfer to the lined tray and spread out in an even layer. Use your hands to pat it down firmly.

Bake for 15–20 minutes, until the top is golden brown but not burnt. Remove from the oven and allow to cool for about 30 minutes.

When it has cooled slightly but is still in the tray, cut into bars. Wrap the tray in cling film and leave in the fridge overnight so that the bars harden.

You can store the whole tray in the fridge or remove the bars and wrap each bar individually in cling film. Store in the fridge and use as needed.

INGREDIENTS

250g agave syrup or honey
200g porridge oats
200g good-quality low-sugar peanut butter
150g raisins
100g skimmed milk powder
100g dried apricots, chopped
100g chopped walnuts (or any chopped nuts)
50g stevia (optional)
50g sesame seeds
3 tbsp melted coconut oil

MAKES 12 BARS

GREEK YOGURT, BERRIES AND CHOCOLATE

100g fresh or frozen berries
170g Greek yogurt
10g 70% dark chocolate,
chopped
1 tsp cocoa powder

SERVES 1

Place the berries in a serving bowl. If using frozen berries, microwave them for 1 minute.

Add the Greek yogurt and chopped chocolate to the bowl. Finish with a sprinkle of cocoa powder.

YOGURT MOUSSE

For those of you who use whey protein in your diet, this is a brilliant but simple snack, but the whey protein isn't essential. The Greek yogurt is high in protein and the nuts provide omega oils, which are great for healthy skin, hair and nails.

Using a fork, whisk the Greek yogurt and whey together, making sure to whisk fast to break up the whey protein and help it blend with the yogurt. Whisking quickly also helps to introduce air into the yogurt to make it light and mousse-like. Stir in the nuts and serve straight away.

INGREDIENTS

150g Greek yogurt
15g chocolate-flavoured whey protein or your favourite flavour (optional)
15g cashew nuts, chopped or whole

SERVES 1

SIDES

'IT IS NOT THE CRITIC WHO COUNTS; NOT THE MAN WHO POINTS OUT HOW THE STRONG MAN STUMBLES, OR WHERE THE DOER OF DEEDS COULD HAVE DONE THEM BETTER. THE CREDIT BELONGS TO THE MAN WHO IS ACTUALLY IN THE ARENA, WHOSE FACE IS MARRED BY DUST AND SWEAT AND BLOOD; WHO STRIVES VALIANTLY; WHO ERRS, WHO COMES SHORT AGAIN AND AGAIN, BECAUSE THERE IS NO EFFORT WITHOUT ERROR AND SHORTCOMING; BUT WHO DOES AC-TUALLY STRIVE TO DO THE DEEDS; WHO KNOWS GREAT ENTHUSIASMS, THE GREAT DEVOTIONS; WHO SPENDS HIMSELF IN A WORTHY CAUSE; WHO AT THE BEST KNOWS IN THE END THE TRIUMPH OF HIGH ACHIEVEMENT, AND WHO AT THE WORST, IF HE FAILS, AT LEAST FAILS WHILE DARING GREATLY, SO THAT HIS PLACE SHALL NEVER BE WITH THOSE COLD AND TIMID SOULS WHO NEITHER KNOW VICTORY NOR DEFEAT.'

THEODORE ROOSEVELT

APPLE AND CELERIAC REMOULADE

This remoulade is a great alternative to coleslaw. Thick and creamy, it works well in salads or with baked potatoes or fish.

Cut the tomatoes in half and scoop out the seeds and watery juices, then finely dice the flesh.

Toss the diced tomatoes, apple, celeriac, gherkins, red onion, dill, parsley and capers together in a large bowl.

In a separate small bowl, whisk together the Greek yogurt, wholegrain mustard, Dijon mustard and vinegar and a pinch of salt and pepper to taste.

Pour the dressing over the apple and celeriac mixture and toss to combine well.

INGREDIENTS

2 small ripe tomatoes
1 sweet, crunchy eating apple,
cored and thinly sliced
¼ celeriac, finely chopped
2 small gherkins
1 small red onion, finely diced
¼ bunch of fresh dill, chopped
¼ bunch of fresh parsley,
chopped
1 tbsp capers, chopped

DRESSING:

200g Greek yogurt
1 tbsp wholegrain mustard
1 tbsp Dijon mustard
1 tsp white wine vinegar
salt and pepper

SERVES 4

RED CABBAGE
COLESLAW

INGREDIENTS

400g red cabbage, finely sliced
3 carrots, peeled and grated
1 red onion, finely diced

DRESSING:

200g Greek yogurt
50ml cider vinegar
1 tbsp Dijon mustard
pinch of caster sugar

SERVES 4

Place the cabbage, carrots and red onion in a large bowl and toss to combine.

In a separate bowl, mix together all the dressing ingredients. Stir through the vegetables until well combined.

CREAMY CHOPPED CAULIFLOWER SALAD

Cauliflower is becoming more and more popular in the kitchen. It has always been a healthy vegetable, but people are getting more adventurous as to how to prepare it. This cauliflower salad is a great side dish to accompany your main.

Whisk together the diced shallot, yogurt, vinegar, caraway seeds and pepper in a large bowl.

Add the chopped lettuce, apple and cauliflower to the bowl and toss together to coat in the dressing.

INGREDIENTS

1 small shallot, finely diced
5 tbsp Greek yogurt
2 tbsp cider vinegar
½ tsp caraway seeds (optional)
¼ tsp freshly ground
black pepper
85g Romaine lettuce, chopped
1 sweet red apple, chopped
½ large head of cauliflower,
chopped

SERVES 6

GRILLED COURGETTES WITH HUMMUS

INGREDIENTS

2 courgettes
2 tbsp melted coconut oil, rapeseed oil or olive oil
hummus (page 63)

SERVES 5

Cut the courgettes in half and then slice lengthways into strips 1cm thick. Place in a bowl with the oil and mix gently so that the courgettes are lightly coated in the oil.

Heat a griddle pan over a medium heat and lightly fry the courgettes, turning them occasionally in order to get nice chargrilled stripes.

Transfer to a plate and spread each grilled courgette with a good dollop of homemade hummus.

BROCCOLI AND CAULIFLOWER GRATIN

One of my favourite comfort foods is a potato gratin.
I always go back for more. I decided to ditch the potato
and replace it with broccoli and cauliflower, which keeps
it lighter and also healthier.

Preheat the oven to 220°C/425°C/gas mark 7. Place the
broccoli and cauliflower in a large bowl with 1 tablespoon
of the olive oil. Toss until they are well coated. Divide
between two baking trays and spread out the florets in an
even layer. Roast the vegetables for 20–25 minutes, until
they are tender and beginning to brown.

Meanwhile, heat 1 tablespoon of oil in a large saucepan
over a medium heat. Add the onion and cook, stirring fre-
quently, for 5–8 minutes, until very soft and golden
brown. Add the flour, salt and pepper and cook, stirring,
for 1 minute more. Pour in the milk and continue to stir,
scraping up any browned bits. Continue to cook, stirring,
until the sauce bubbles and thickens enough to coat the
back of the spoon. Remove the sauce from the heat.

When the vegetables are done, remove them from the
oven and preheat the grill.

Transfer half of the vegetables to a grill-safe baking dish.
Spread half of the sauce over the vegetables, then add the
remaining vegetables and top with the remaining sauce.

Combine the oats and cheese with the remaining 1 tablespoon of oil in a small bowl. Spread the topping over the
vegetable mixture in the dish. Place under the grill until
the gratin is bubbling and beginning to brown on top, but
watch it closely so it doesn't burn. Leave to cool for 5
minutes before serving.

INGREDIENTS

1 head of broccoli, trimmed and
cut into 3cm florets
½ head of cauliflower, trimmed
and cut into 3cm florets
3 tbsp extra virgin olive oil
1 medium onion, thinly sliced
3 tbsp plain flour
¾ tsp salt
¼ tsp white or black pepper
500ml low-fat milk
100g porridge oats
(not jumbo oats)
50g freshly grated Parmesan

SERVES 6

ROASTED BUTTERNUT SQUASH

1 butternut squash, peeled,
deseeded and chopped
into 4cm cubes
1 tsp olive oil
1 garlic clove, crushed
salt and pepper
small bunch of fresh sage leaves,
chopped
300g Greek yogurt
200g freshly grated Parmesan

SERVES 2

This is a great side dish to accompany so many meals. Butternut squash is great to cook with; the only hard part is the chopping. It was often overlooked and I've only just started to use it myself, but it's a great low-calorie carbohydrate to have in your diet and it's something I now buy every week.

Roasting with Greek yogurt sounds a little odd, but it adds so much flavour to the squash along with the garlic and Parmesan.

Preheat the oven to 180°C/350°F/gas mark 4.

Place the chopped butternut squash in a roasting tray, drizzle with the olive oil and add the crushed garlic. Season with salt and pepper. Toss all the ingredients together and roast in the oven for 20 minutes.

Remove the squash from the oven and mix in the sage leaves and yogurt. Sprinkle over the grated cheese and put it back in the oven for a further 20 minutes, until the butternut squash has nicely roasted edges.

> **'CHAMPIONS AREN'T MADE IN THE GYM. CHAMPIONS ARE MADE FROM SOMETHING THEY HAVE DEEP INSIDE THEM – A DESIRE, A DREAM, A VISION. THEY HAVE TO HAVE THE SKILL, AND THE WILL. BUT THE WILL MUST BE STRONGER THAN THE SKILL.'**
>
> MUHAMMAD ALI

It's amazing how many people define lunch as a sandwich. I recently gave a nutritional talk and a member of the audience couldn't get his head around having a lunch with no bread. There is a lot more out there than two slices of bread and some processed deli meat!

Do you ever have a big meal at lunchtime and then get tired and lethargic later in the afternoon and feel like you need a pick-me-up such as a biscuit or chocolate? Eating too much at lunchtime or not eating enough good stuff can set you up for an unproductive afternoon and evening. It's back to that old slogan: breakfast like a king, lunch like a queen and dine like a pauper.

Lunch was extremely important for me when I was running full time, as it was essentially a post-training recovery. Some people think that because you are training hard, you can get away with eating anything you want. That's true, but only up to a certain point. Yes, you are burning a lot of calories so therefore you can eat more calories, but the focus should be on quality, not quantity.

I liked my routine and the easiest thing was to stick to what I knew, so my lunch for a number of months was roughly the same, day after day. Staples included turkey or chicken for protein, quinoa or couscous for carbohydrate, feta cheese and half an avocado for essential good fats and, finally, a mixed salad and vegetables. It might sound boring, but I knew it was the right stuff to be eating for optimal recovery and to maintain a good weight.

As I got older and learned more about food, I began to change things around, but I always kept the same principles in mind: real food and balance. The aim was to add a little more variety to my lunch and not to keep eating the same things over and over.

In this chapter you will find plenty of options for lunches, including some good ideas for people with busy schedules, in the office, on the road and also for those days when you might have a little more time to prepare a lunch.

ON THE ROAD

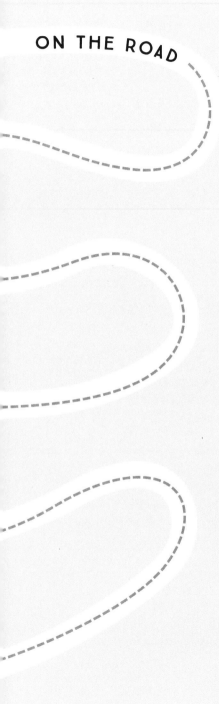

Having lunch on the road is tough. In one of my roles after I retired, I spent some time on the road and found it very difficult to eat well. I would go long durations without eating and then need to stop at a filling station. If I was hungry when I walked into the shop to pay for diesel, I always wound up buying a fresh muffin or croissant. I would then sit in the car for another few hours overanalysing why I had bought it. Over time, I learned to be prepared.

- I would only stop at places where I knew I could get good food.
- I would always ask for salad in a bowl, not in between two slices of bread.
- I would spend a little more time in the shop trying to find healthy options and not just grab and go.
- I would try to cook a little extra the night before and have that for lunch the following day.
- Nuts became my companion in the passenger seat for those sudden bolts of hunger.
- I would also have a large bottle of water beside me to sip from.

It wasn't easy, but I had more energy throughout the day if I stuck to these guidelines and had a proper lunch, no matter where I was.

ROAST CHICKEN AND CHORIZO SOUP

INGREDIENTS

1 tsp olive oil
50g chorizo, sliced
4 medium carrots, peeled
and chopped
2 onions, chopped
1 tbsp fresh thyme leaves,
roughly chopped
1½ litres chicken stock
400g leftover roast chicken,
shredded and skin removed
150g frozen peas
salt and pepper

SERVES 4

If you roast a chicken on a Sunday, this is a great way to use the leftovers to make the roast go a long way. I love chorizo – it adds so much flavour and goes great with chicken.

Heat the oil in a deep saucepan over a medium heat. Add the chorizo, carrots, onions and thyme and fry gently for 15 minutes, until the vegetables have softened. Stir in the stock, cover with a lid and bring to a boil. Reduce the heat and simmer for 15 minutes.

Add the chicken, then purée the soup with a stick blender. Add the peas and season with salt and pepper. Simmer for 5 minutes, until the peas have heated through. Ladle into warmed bowls and serve.

RED LENTIL, CHICKPEA AND CHILLI SOUP

There is nothing better than a bowl of warm soup on a cold day, and with a hint of chilli you get an extra punch. I'm a big of fan of protein and I try to have a good source of it in every meal. By using lentils I'm still getting a hit of protein while giving my body a break from animal protein. It's important to eat different sources of protein, as this will provide you with an array of nutrients and minerals.

Heat a large saucepan over a medium heat and dry-fry the cumin seeds and chilli flakes for 1 minute, until they start to jump around the pan and release their aromas.

Add the oil to the saucepan, then add the onion and cook for 5 minutes, until the onion has started to soften. Stir in the tomatoes, lentils and stock and bring to the boil. Reduce the heat and simmer for 15 minutes, until the lentils have softened.

Whizz the contents of the saucepan with a stick blender or in a food processor until it's a rough purée. Add the chickpeas and heat gently over a low heat. Season well with salt and pepper.

Serve in warmed bowls with a dollop of yogurt and fresh coriander.

INGREDIENTS

1 tsp cumin seeds
small pinch of chilli flakes
1 tbsp olive oil
½ red onion, chopped
200g canned tomatoes,
whole or chopped
70g red split lentils
400ml vegetable stock or water
100g cooked or tinned chickpeas
(rinsed and drained if tinned)
salt and pepper
2 tbsp Greek yogurt, to garnish
small bunch of fresh coriander,
roughly chopped, to garnish

SERVES 2

MUSHROOM SOUP

Growing up I hated mushrooms; they wouldn't get near my plate. However, I have grown to love them and the various types all have distinctive tastes. Combining them together brings them all to life, resulting in a really tasty and easy to make soup.

Heat the olive oil in a saucepan over a medium heat. Add the chopped onion and leek and cook for 10 minutes, until soft. Stir in all the mushrooms.

Dissolve the stock cube in the boiling water. Add the stock to the pan and simmer until the mushrooms are cooked and soft.

Using a hand blender, blend the soup until it reaches the desired consistency. Season with a pinch of salt and pepper and serve.

INGREDIENTS

1 tbsp olive oil
1 onion, chopped
1 leek, chopped
50g button mushrooms, chopped
50g chestnut mushrooms, chopped
50g Portobello mushrooms, chopped
50g oyster mushrooms
1 vegetable stock cube
200ml boiling water
sea salt and pepper

SERVES 2

SLOW-COOKED BEEF SOUP

You can bang this recipe into the slow cooker as you are making your breakfast and when you arrive home from work you'll have a fantastic soup to tuck into, with slow-cooked beef so tender that it just falls apart. Or you can have it for your lunch that same day with plenty left over for the following few days too.

Add all the ingredients to a slow cooker. Cover and cook for 4 hours on high or 8 hours on low.

When cooked, blend with a stick blender until it's a smooth consistency. If it's too thick, add a little water. Another option is not to blend the soup at all and serve it as a beef broth.

Serve with slices of sourdough bread.

INGREDIENTS

500g cubed stewing beef
6 carrots, peeled and chopped
5 celery sticks, chopped
2 onions, chopped
2 bay leaves
600ml beef stock
2 tsp garlic powder or 2 garlic cloves, crushed
1 tsp cracked black pepper
pinch of salt

SERVES 4

CHICKEN AND SPINACH WRAP

Lunch can be tough. A lot of people don't have time to cook and are looking for something quick and healthy. Every meal should be balanced and include elements from all the food groups. I like using wraps, as they are lighter than paninis or ciabatta, and I pack them full of goodness. The avocado purée is full of healthy fats, plus it makes the wrap moist and appetising. Another good wrap filling is turkey and the homemade coleslaw on page 85.

Put the avocado in a bowl and mash with a fork. Stir in the tomato and garlic purées and mix together well.

Lay the wrap out on the worktop and spread the mashed avocado down the middle of the wrap. Cover with the chicken and spinach. Finish by adding the diced pepper, sliced mozzarella and chopped basil. Drizzle with olive oil and fold the wrap up tightly. Cut in half on the diagonal and serve.

INGREDIENTS

½ ripe avocado
1 tbsp tomato purée
1 tsp garlic purée
1 wholegrain wrap
150g cooked chicken, sliced
small handful of spinach
½ red pepper, diced
50g mozzarella, sliced
a few fresh basil leaves, chopped
1 tsp olive oil

SERVES 1

CREAMY
TUNA SALAD

INGREDIENTS

1 x 120g tin of tuna, drained
100g Greek yogurt
80g cucumber, finely chopped
2 spring onions, chopped
1 celery stick, chopped
½ apple, finely chopped
a few fresh chives, chopped
large handful of mixed salad
leaves, such as spinach and rocket
½ ripe avocado, chopped
drizzle of balsamic vinegar
15g shelled pistachio nuts or
cashew nuts

SERVES 1

This is one of my favourite lunches. When I make this salad for other people, they are always surprised when I tell them I make it with Greek yogurt as an alternative to mayonnaise. It's really easy to make and is thick, crunchy and filling. I always make a big bowl by doubling the ingredients and it gets me by for a few days.

Tinned tuna is a great store cupboard stand-by, but don't eat it too often, as it can be high in mercury. Once every ten days or so is fine.

———————————————————————

Place the tuna, Greek yogurt, cucumber, spring onions, celery, apple and chives in a large bowl and mix together.

Prepare a bed of salad leaves and avocado on a plate and drizzle with balsamic vinegar. Place the tuna on top of the salad and garnish with the nuts.

BLT SALAD

INGREDIENTS

2 slices of bacon
½ ripe avocado
30g feta cheese
small handful of cherry tomatoes
large handful of
mixed salad leaves
2 tsp lemon juice
1 tsp olive oil
15g pine nuts

SERVES 1

You can prepare this the night before or in the morning before you leave for work or hit the road.

_____

Cook the bacon under a hot grill until crisp, turning it every few minutes so it cooks evenly. When the bacon is done, transfer it to a plate lined with kitchen paper to soak up any excess grease, then chop the bacon into pieces.

Chop the avocado and feta cheese into small cubes. Quarter the tomatoes and place in a bowl along with the avocado, feta and bacon.

Add the mixed leaves and toss with a good squeeze of lemon juice and a drizzle of extra virgin olive oil. Top with pine nuts.

CHARGRILLED CHICKEN, COURGETTE AND ROCKET SALAD

Dressings make a dish, but when eating out I always ask for the dressing on the side because a lot of them are high in calories. But not all dressings have to be unhealthy. You can bring three simple salad ingredients to life by cooking and slicing them in a different way and adding a homemade dressing.

Heat a griddle pan over a medium heat. Drizzle the chicken with the olive oil and season both sides with salt and pepper. Cook the chicken on the griddle pan for about 7 minutes, turning once, until the chicken has nice chargrill marks and is cooked through. Remove the chicken to a cutting board and allow to rest.

To make the vinaigrette, combine the diced shallot, lemon zest and juice, capers and white wine vinegar in a small bowl. Slowly pour in the olive oil while whisking continuously, until thoroughly combined. Season to taste with salt and pepper.

To prepare the salad, hold the stem of the courgettes. Using a vegetable peeler, peel thin ribbons until you get almost halfway through. Flip the courgette and repeat on the other side. Discard the inner core.

Assemble the salad by combining the courgette ribbons, tomatoes and rocket in a large bowl. Drizzle with half the vinaigrette and gently toss with your hands, being careful not to break the courgette ribbons. Divide the salad evenly between four plates.

Slice the chicken and place on top of the salad. Drizzle with the remaining vinaigrette.

INGREDIENTS

500g chicken breast, flattened
with a mallet to 1cm thick
1 tbsp olive oil
salt and pepper
2 small courgettes
100g cherry tomatoes, halved
75g rocket

VINAIGRETTE:

1 shallot, finely diced
1 lemon, zest and juice
1 tbsp capers, roughly chopped
2 tsp white wine vinegar
3 tbsp olive oil
salt and pepper

SERVES 4

PROSCIUTTO AND CHICKEN CAESAR SALAD

INGREDIENTS

6 slices of prosciutto
2 large chicken breast fillets
2 tsp olive oil
3 heads of Cos lettuce
50g mixed seeds

DRESSING:

2 garlic cloves, crushed
75ml white wine
1 tbsp white wine vinegar
2 egg yolks
1 anchovy fillet
100g Parmesan, grated or flaked
150ml extra virgin olive oil
2 tsp Dijon mustard
salt and pepper

SERVES 4

The classic Caesar salad is great – until it's smothered in dressing and accompanied by croutons. I've got rid of the croutons and added seeds for crunch. I've also made my own dressing that is full of flavour and a lot healthier.

To make the dressing, bring the garlic, white wine and vinegar to a boil in a medium saucepan. Reduce the heat and simmer for about 5 minutes, until the garlic has softened. Leave to cool.

Combine the wine, vinegar and garlic with the egg yolks, anchovy and Parmesan in a mixing bowl. Blend with a hand blender or food processor until smooth. Drizzle in the oil in a thin, steady stream, continuing to blend all the time. Do not add the oil too quickly, otherwise it could split and curdle. Stir in the mustard and add seasoning to taste.

Preheat the grill to high. Place the prosciutto on a baking sheet and place under the grill for 3–4 minutes, until crisp.

Butterfly the chicken breasts by slicing them horizontally without cutting all the way through, creating one large flat piece of chicken when opened. Season with pepper and brush with olive oil.

Heat a griddle pan until hot. Place the chicken breasts on it and cook them for 10–15 minutes, turning once, until cooked through. Remove the chicken to a chopping board and cut into slices.

Separate the leaves from the lettuce, cut into chunky pieces and place in a bowl. Add the prosciutto and seeds to the bowl and pour over most of the dressing. Toss to combine. Transfer to four plates and divide the sliced chicken evenly between them. Drizzle a little more dressing over and serve.

SPICY BUTTERY TURKEY WITH FETA AND GIANT COUSCOUS SALAD

Turkey, feta and couscous are staples in my diet, so I'm always trying new ways to eat them. Varying your ingredients can give you completely different flavours and as a result, a different meal. In this recipe I mix together butter, chilli and garlic to make a great-tasting paste that adds so much flavour to the turkey. Couscous and quinoa are healthy, slow-releasing carbohydrates that by themselves are bland, but stirring them through some simple ingredients can give them a new lease of life.

Cook the couscous or quinoa as per the packet instructions and drain well. Meanwhile, mix the butter, chilli and garlic into a paste.

Toss the turkey in 1 tablespoon of olive oil along with a pinch of salt and pepper.

Heat a griddle pan over a medium heat until it's smoking hot. Cook the turkey on the hot pan for 5 minutes on each side, until cooked through. Transfer to a plate, dot with the spicy butter and set aside to let it melt. Once the butter has melted, slice the turkey.

Tip the onion, tomatoes, olives, feta and mint into a bowl. Stir through the cooked couscous or quinoa along with the remaining tablespoon of olive oil, lemon juice and zest and seeds, and season well.

Place a handful of mixed leaves on four plates, divide the salad between them and put the sliced turkey on top, drizzled with any buttery turkey juices.

INGREDIENTS

200g giant couscous or quinoa
30g butter, softened
1 fresh red chilli, deseeded and
finely chopped
1 garlic clove, crushed
4 turkey breast steaks
2 tbsp olive oil
salt and pepper
1 red onion, finely sliced
300g ripe vine tomatoes,
roughly chopped
100g black olives
100g feta cheese, crumbled
small bunch of fresh mint leaves,
chopped
juice and zest of ½ lemon
30g mixed seeds
4 good handfuls of mixed leaves

SERVES 4

CHICKEN, QUINOA AND MANGO SALAD

INGREDIENTS

60g quinoa
1 tsp coconut oil
1 medium chicken breast,
chopped into bite-sized chunks
½ ripe mango, cubed
½ red pepper, chopped
½ red onion, chopped
handful of mixed salad leaves
handful of fresh mint leaves,
chopped
juice of ½ lemon
15g cashew nuts, chopped
1 tbsp Udo's Choice
ultimate oil blend

SERVES 1

I was once referred to as the quinoa king and I don't want to let anyone down, so I've added it to chicken and mango to make a fresh-tasting summer salad. Putting fruit in a salad is a good way of getting more antioxidants into your diet, which are needed for recovery from exercise, for boosting your immune system and for good general health. I also use Udo's Choice ultimate oil blend as a dressing as it is a great way to get healthy good fats into my body to maintain health, aid recovery and boost energy levels.

Cook the quinoa as per the packet instructions and drain well.

Melt the coconut oil in a frying pan over a medium heat. Add the chicken and cook for 10 minutes, stirring occasionally, until it's cooked through.

Combine the cooked quinoa, mango, red pepper, red onion, salad leaves and chopped mint in a bowl and drizzle the lemon juice and Udo's oil over them. Mix in the chicken and sprinkle with the chopped cashew nuts.

THAI CHICKEN CUPS

This is a really tasty lunch that's full of flavour and all the goodness you need. Thai paste is made of all-natural ingredients, so it's guilt free and great to cook with. Be careful not to add too much, though, as it can pack a punch!

Instead of using a slice of bread to serve, I use a Gem lettuce leaf. Most people simply use a slice of bread out of pure habit, so if you're looking to cut down on carbs, lettuce cups are a good alternative.

Melt the Thai curry paste and coconut oil in a large frying pan over a medium heat. Add the chopped chicken breasts and the lime zest and fry for 10 minutes, until the chicken is light brown and cooked through. Remove from the heat and leave to cool.

Meanwhile, put the lime juice, yogurt and coriander in a large bowl and mix together well. Add the cooled cooked chicken to the bowl and stir to coat.

To assemble the cups, spoon the chicken into the lettuce leaves. Top with some onion, carrot and pepper and sprinkle with crushed cashew nuts.

INGREDIENTS

2 tsp Thai red curry paste
1 tsp coconut oil
200g chicken breast fillets, chopped
zest and juice of 1 lime
125g Greek yogurt
handful of fresh coriander leaves, roughly chopped
8 Gem lettuce leaves
1 small red onion, diced
1 medium carrot, peeled and grated
1 small red pepper, thinly sliced
25g cashew nuts, crushed

SERVES 2

TURKEY, FETA AND AVOCADO QUINOA SALAD

I ate this dish religiously for years. Quick and easy, it's got everything you need. For variety I use turkey, but chicken is fine too. Turkey is a lean protein and tends to be cheaper than chicken. It's always a good idea to try different protein sources, as each type brings much-needed minerals and vitamins to a dish.

Cook the quinoa according to the packet instructions and drain well.

Melt the coconut oil in a large frying pan over a medium heat. Add the diced red pepper and fry for 4–5 minutes, until softened slightly. Add the turkey to the pan and season with salt and pepper. Cook for 10 minutes, just to brown the turkey. Add the tomato and garlic purées along with the water. Stir well. If it looks too dry, add a little more water. Add the spinach and continue to cook for a further minute, stirring continuously, until it has wilted slightly.

To plate up, place the mixed leaves on a plate and cover with the turkey. Finish by topping with crumbled feta cheese, sliced avocado and the torn basil leaves. Serve the quinoa on the side.

INGREDIENTS

50g quinoa
1 tsp coconut oil
½ red pepper, diced
150g turkey breast steaks, chopped into bite-sized chunks
salt and pepper
1 tbsp tomato purée
1 tsp garlic purée
50ml water
good handful of spinach
handful of mixed salad leaves
50g feta cheese, crumbled
½ ripe avocado, sliced
a few fresh basil leaves, torn

SERVES 1

MIXED BEAN SALAD

INGREDIENTS

2 x 400g cans of mixed beans,
drained and rinsed
250g cherry tomatoes, halved
2 spring onions, finely sliced
1 small bunch of fresh
parsley leaves

DRESSING:

2 tbsp olive oil
1 tbsp red wine vinegar
1 tsp wholegrain mustard

SERVES 4

Tinned beans are essential in a balanced diet and are a must-have in any cupboard. They are cheap, they have a long shelf-life, they are very versatile and quick to use. Beans are a great source of protein and can be added to loads of dishes. Here, they are the main ingredient in a salad.

Combine the drained mixed beans, cherry tomatoes, spring onions and parsley leaves in a large bowl.

In a separate small bowl, whisk together the oil, vinegar and mustard.

Add the dressing to the bowl of beans. Toss to combine and serve straight away.

SPANISH OMELETTE

INGREDIENTS

1 tsp coconut oil or rapeseed oil
150g sweet potato, peeled
and finely diced
½ onion, chopped
½ pepper, diced (add as much
colour as you wish)
80g mushrooms, chopped
100g tinned chopped tomatoes
handful of fresh spinach
1 tsp paprika (optional)
4 medium free-range eggs,
beaten
salt and pepper
30g feta cheese, crumbled

SERVES 1

This has to be one of my all-time favourite meals. It's quick, healthy and has everything you need on one plate. By increasing the quantities and cooking it for a little longer, it becomes a great dish to share.

This recipe was a staple in my diet, week in and week out, and it never gets boring. By simply adding in new ingredients or replacing existing ones, you get a completely different take on it. Sometimes I add chorizo or sweetcorn and I've even been known to replace the sweet potato with quinoa.

Preheat the grill to a medium–high heat.

Melt the oil in a medium ovenproof frying pan over a medium heat. Pan-fry the diced sweet potatoes for 3–4 minutes, until starting to soften. The smaller you chop the sweet potato, the quicker it will cook. Add the chopped onion and let it sweat for another 2 minutes. Add the pepper and mushrooms and fry for 3 minutes, stirring continuously. Pour in the chopped tomatoes, add the spinach and the paprika, if using, and mix well.

Pour the beaten eggs over the vegetables in the pan. Do not mix, but rather tip the pan so the eggs run evenly across the whole pan. Season with salt and pepper.

Cook for a further 3–4 minutes, until the bottom begins to set, making sure the base doesn't burn. Place the pan under the grill for about 5 minutes to cook the top. Add the crumbled feta at this point. The omelette is done when the eggs have completely set.

Tip the omelette out onto a plate and cut into wedges to serve.

QUICHE

Every deli in the country has a quiche in the fridge. The filling, which is generally made from eggs, a protein source, and vegetables, is great, but unfortunately the pastry base doesn't have great nutritional value. In my recipe I use oats, seeds and ground almonds for the base and it works really well. You can also swap the Cheddar cheese for a different cheese if you'd prefer.

Preheat the oven to 190°C/375°F/gas mark 5. Grease a quiche dish with butter.

Rinse the lentils and place in a large saucepan of boiling water. Simmer for 15 minutes, until softened. Drain well and put them back in the saucepan.

Meanwhile, melt the coconut oil in a frying pan over a medium heat. Add the onion and cook for 5 minutes, until it's starting to soften. Lightly fry the chicken and bacon for 10 minutes, until both are cooked through and the onion has softened. Set aside.

Mix the ground almonds, oats, sesame seeds and some salt and pepper with the lentils in the saucepan. Beat one egg in a separate small bowl and stir it into the oat and lentil mixture. The mixture will bind together, but it won't be anything like pastry. Allow to cool slightly, then use your hands to press the mixture into the base and up the sides of the quiche dish.

Carefully position the chicken, bacon, onion and vegetables in the bottom of the quiche. Beat the three remaining eggs, Greek yogurt and some black pepper together in a separate bowl and pour over the filling in the quiche dish. Sprinkle with the cheese.

Bake for 35 minutes, until the filling is set. Serve hot or cold.

INGREDIENTS

1 tsp butter, for greasing
50g red lentils
1 tsp coconut oil
1 small onion, chopped
2 large chicken breast fillets, chopped into bite-sized chunks
3 rashers, chopped
70g ground almonds
50g porridge oats
30g sesame seeds
salt and pepper
4 medium free-range eggs
200g mixed vegetables, such as red pepper and courgette, finely diced
200g Greek yogurt
50g Cheddar cheese, grated

SERVES 4

ck back i
e running for
orld indoors

one s
to Ry
playi

Athletics

[...]na
[...]ey

YEAR after he shocked
e international athletics
orld by winning the Euro-
pe [...] indoor 400m title,
[...] David Gillick has
[...] another surprise
[...] a contender
['s World
[...]ships.
[...]usly
[...]
[...] as

**David Gillick has been
pencilled in to travel**

[...]rkansas. Cork sprint hur-
[...] Derval O'Rourke, who
[...]ed the national 60m
[...] record twice
[...] is the team's
[...]me.
[...] is James
[...]oked most
[...] He had
[...]500m
[...] of

PACE:
[...]llick
[...]old

Y MIRROR, Monday, June 11, 2007

ORLD RANKING BOOST AFTE[...]

Golf

**Karl
MacGinty**

TOM LEHMAN'S dream of
playing in his own US team
at The K Club took a step
closer to reality yesterday
when his name popped-up
at No 10 in the American
Ryder Cup rankings.
People on this side of the
Atlantic might think it crazy
for anyone to take on the
dual role of Ryder Cup play-
er-captain in the modern era.
European skipper Ian
Woosnam has said he cer-
tainly wouldn't consider it,
while Bernhard Langer, who
led the massacre at Oakland
Hills in 2004, has advised his
[...]nd Lehman not to try.
[...] Lehman's the pioneer-
[...] and, having dis-
[...] subject with him
[...]imes in the past
[...] clear he's rel-
[...]nge.
[...] US team
[...]on't be
[...]seven

SPAR 4
324
BIRMINGHAM 2007

**Du[...]
sta
strid[...]
top in**

H
[...]
sh
an
the

im
sin

sport

Irish Independent
Wednesday 30
May 2007

'Galway can't win title'
[...]hsent hero Joe Canning believes
[...]way can't regain the Liam McCarthy
this year. Pages 2-3

Tee to Green supplement
Don't miss your comprehensive
eight-page guide to all that's
happening in Irish golf. Pages 9-16

Eddie bites back
Eddie O'Sullivan has hit
back over claims Ireland
used 'roughhouse tactics'

5

www.independent.ie

rint superstars are all
o take on the World

Sport

→ in brief

Brooke on mend
following surgery

RUGBY: Former All Blac[...]
ward Zinzan Brooke[...]
make a comple[...]
after under[...]
head

STUFFED PEPPERS

INGREDIENTS

150g couscous
125ml vegetable stock
60g frozen peas
2 red peppers
olive oil
80g crumbled feta cheese
60g sweetcorn
1 ripe tomato, chopped
1 spring onion, finely chopped
1 egg, beaten
4 fresh basil leaves, chopped
salt and pepper

SERVES 4

A lot of people find it hard to eat healthily and cheaply at lunchtime. If you bring lunch to work, couscous should be part of your ammunition. All you need to do is add boiling water or stock, leave it for 5 minutes and it's done. I'm big into grains and I try to vary them as much as possible. This recipe can be prepared the night before or in the morning before you leave for work. It will also last for a couple of days in the fridge, so you get more out of spending a little time on the prep!

Preheat the oven to 180°C/350°F/gas mark 4. Line a baking tray with parchment paper.

Place the couscous in a large bowl. Boil the stock and stir it through the couscous. Cover the bowl with cling film and set aside for 5 minutes, until all the stock has been absorbed.

Meanwhile, cook the frozen peas in boiling water for 5 minutes or microwave for 2 minutes. Drain well.

Cut each pepper in half lengthwise, scoop out the seeds and discard them. Place the pepper halves on the lined tray.

Fluff up the couscous with a fork and add a small drizzle of olive oil. Stir in the peas, feta, sweetcorn, chopped tomato, spring onion, beaten egg and basil and mix well. Season with salt and pepper.

Spoon the couscous into the pepper halves. Cook in the oven for 25 minutes, until the peppers have softened.

CHICKEN SOBA NOODLES

Soba is Japanese for buckwheat, but nowadays soba tends to refer to any thin noodle. I always try to use buckwheat noodles as they're nutritious, low in calories and great for people who are sensitive to wheat or other grains. Buckwheat isn't a type of wheat – it's actually a fruit seed related to rhubarb.

This dish is great at home or on the road and tastes great served either warm or cold.

_____

Cook the noodles according to the packet instructions. Have your colander ready in the sink and prepare a bowl of cold water. When the noodles are cooked, drain and promptly dump them in the cold water, then drain again. This helps get rid of excess starch.

Once the noodles have been drained for the second time, warm them by heating 1 tsp of sesame oil in a frying pan over a low heat, then add the noodles and the rest of the ingredients. Toss together to combine.

INGREDIENTS

60g soba noodles
(buckwheat noodles)
1 tsp sesame oil
150g cooked chicken, chopped,
sliced or shredded (or you could
use cooked sliced beef)
5 mangetout, finely sliced
1 small carrot, peeled into
ribbon-like strips
½ red pepper, sliced
½ fresh red chilli, deseeded
and finely diced
1 garlic clove, crushed
1 tbsp sesame seeds
1 tsp lime juice
1 tsp soy sauce

SERVES 1

CRUNCHY GRILLED COD WITH PESTO

INGREDIENTS

80g Greek yogurt
25g pesto (made with olive oil rather than sunflower oil)
1 x 100g cod fillet
100g ripe tomatoes, chopped
½ yellow pepper, chopped
15g crushed cashew nuts
10g grated Parmesan

SERVES 1

A lot of people have some breaded cod in the freezer. Fish is a healthy addition to your diet, but the breaded coating surrounding the cod brings down the nutritional value. However, I like breaded cod as much as the next person, so I've come up with my own. The crushed nuts give a great crunch and the sauce adds lots of flavour.

The portion size given here is for one person, so just increase the quantities as needed.

Preheat the grill to a medium–high heat.

Mix the Greek yogurt and pesto together to form a paste.

Place the cod on a baking tray with the chopped tomatoes and pepper. Using a tablespoon, spread a thin layer of the pesto mixture across the fillet to cover it.

Grill for 10–15 minutes, until the fish is cooked through, but make sure the sauce on top of the fish doesn't brown or burn. It can be hard to control grill temperatures, so do keep an eye on it.

After 10–15 minutes, take the fish out of the grill and sprinkle the crushed cashew nuts over the cod. Place back under the grill on a medium heat for 5 minutes to crisp up the cashews.

Take the cod out of the grill again and sprinkle the grated Parmesan over it. Grill for 2 minutes more to melt the cheese.

Serve hot with the remaining Greek yogurt and pesto sauce, the roast veg and some roasted sweet potatoes.

SALMON FILLET WITH ASPARAGUS SALAD AND TABBOULEH

This was one of my winning dishes in *Celebrity MasterChef Ireland*. There are plenty of ways to cook salmon, but I went with pan-frying it, followed by the oven. I usually grill salmon with the skin on and then I take it off and grill the other side of the skin to get it nice and crispy. You can also use coconut oil to fry, as it's a lot healthier and has a higher smoking point than olive oil.

Some of these foods are staples in my diet, which can get boring sometimes, but this dish puts a bit of life back into them. It's got lots of colour, flavour and depth and is highly nutritious. Salmon is full of protein and good omega fats, while quinoa is a good source of carbs and protein along with minerals and vitamins.

This is a more complicated recipe which requires a little more preparation time, but we're all entitled to a posh lunch now and again.

To make the tabbouleh, cook the quinoa as per the packet instructions. Once cooked, fluff it up with a fork before adding it to the other ingredients.

Place the diced tomato, coriander, mint and capers in a large bowl. Add the quinoa, then stir in the white wine vinegar and a pinch of salt. Set aside to let the flavours blend together while you prepare the salmon and the salad.

CONTINUED ON PAGE 130

INGREDIENTS

1 tsp oil
180g salmon fillet
a good pinch of salt
4 asparagus spears,
each chopped into 3 pieces
4 thin slices of fennel
¼ orange, peeled and
cut into segments
1 radish, thinly sliced
small handful of green olives
small bunch of fresh parsley,
finely chopped
2 tbsp capers

TABBOULEH:

100g quinoa
1 small ripe tomato, finely diced
4 sprigs of fresh coriander,
finely chopped
4 sprigs of fresh mint,
finely chopped
1 tbsp capers
1 tsp white wine vinegar
pinch of salt

SERVES 1

Heat the oil in an ovenproof frying pan over a medium heat. Salt the skin side of the salmon and fry in the pan, skin side down, for 5–6 minutes. Put a bit of pressure on the salmon to keep the skin from curling up. Turn the salmon over and give it another 2–3 minutes, until cooked through.

Meanwhile, blanch the asparagus in boiling water for 5 minutes, until tender, then drain well and plunge into a bowl of cold water to stop it cooking and to retain its bright green colour.

Transfer to a large bowl and toss with the fennel slices, orange segments, sliced radish, olives, parsley and capers to make the salad.

To serve, assemble the salad on a plate. Place the salmon on top and serve some tabbouleh alongside.

THAI FISHCAKES

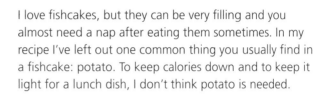

I love fishcakes, but they can be very filling and you almost need a nap after eating them sometimes. In my recipe I've left out one common thing you usually find in a fishcake: potato. To keep calories down and to keep it light for a lunch dish, I don't think potato is needed.

Put the fish, prawns, curry paste, coriander and a pinch of salt in a food processor and blend until it forms a paste. Add the green beans and blend at a higher speed. Refrigerate if you are not cooking the fishcakes immediately.

Place the chopped cucumbers in a bowl. Add the chillies, vinegar and water and mix together. Set aside.

With greased or wet hands, shape the fish mixture into two small cakes. Heat the oil in a large frying pan over a low heat. Fry the cakes for 10 minutes on each side, until firm and cooked through.

Prepare the green salad and add the sliced peppers. Place on a serving plate and drizzle with the balsamic vinegar.

As soon as the fishcakes are cooked, place them on the serving plate with the salad. Add the cucumbers to the plate and garnish with the cashews and coriander. Add a dollop of Greek yogurt as a dip. Serve while the fishcakes are hot.

INGREDIENTS

100g smoked or tinned salmon
50g cooked prawns
½ tsp Thai red or panang curry paste
a few fresh coriander leaves
pinch of salt
25g green beans, topped and tailed
2 tsp coconut oil
40g Greek yogurt

CUCUMBERS
(PER PERSON):

80g cucumber, finely chopped
½ small red or green chilli, de-seeded and finely chopped
1 tsp white wine vinegar
1 tsp water
10g cashew nuts, chopped
a few fresh coriander leaves, chopped

GREEN SALAD:

160g salad, to include any of the following: lettuce, spinach or rocket leaves, celery, spring onions
50g mixed peppers, sliced
2 tsp balsamic vinegar

MAKES 2 FISHCAKES

SALMON RICE PAPER ROLLS

INGREDIENTS

60g bulgur wheat
2 tsp soy sauce
2 tsp lime juice
6 fresh mint leaves, chopped
120g smoked or tinned salmon
6 large rice paper wrappers
1 onion, thinly sliced
1 small carrot, peeled and cut into
matchsticks
½ medium red pepper, thinly
sliced
80g Greek yogurt
50g sweet chilli sauce

MAKES 6 ROLLS

I love spring rolls, but deep-frying isn't too healthy, I'm afraid. Using rice paper, fresh vegetables and of course not frying them makes them a healthy snack, though. Packed with fresh ingredients, it's a versatile and quick dish to have for lunch, especially if you use smoked or tinned salmon as I do here. You could also use brown rice, quinoa or couscous instead of the bulgur wheat.

Cook the bulgur wheat as per the packet instructions. Leave to cool.

When the bulgur is cool, add the soy sauce, lime juice and chopped mint. If using tinned salmon, add it at this point. Stir to combine.

Half-fill a large, shallow dish with warm water. Place one rice paper in the water just until soft. Transfer to your work surface.

If using smoked salmon, place one slice along one edge of the rice paper. Top with 1 tablespoon of the bulgur wheat mixture and some onion, carrot and red pepper. Roll up tightly, folding in the top and bottom edges to enclose the filling.

Cover the finished rolls with a clean damp tea towel to prevent them drying out. Repeat with the remaining rice paper and filling to make five more rolls.

For the dip, mix together the Greek yogurt and sweet chilli sauce in a small bowl.

Eat straight away or refrigerate the rolls in an airtight container for up to two days. Serve with the dip on the side.

DINNER

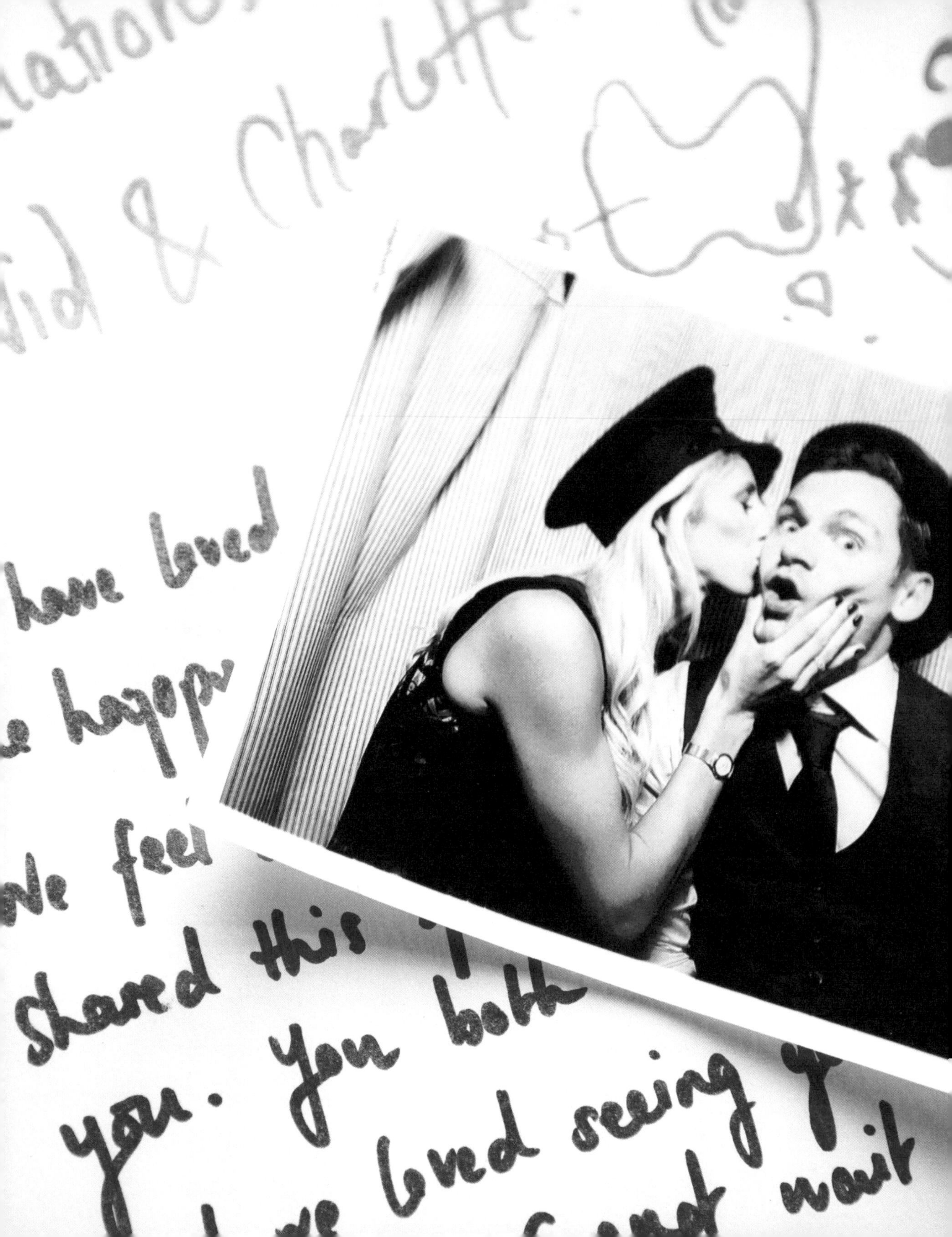
have loved
shared this
you. You both
loved seeing

'RESENTMENT IS LIKE DRINKING POISON AND THEN HOPING IT WILL KILL YOUR ENEMIES.'

NELSON MANDELA

When I was training full time, my day would finish somewhere between 4 and 5 p.m. Charlotte was working full time too, so I was the one left to sort out the dinner.

I didn't mind taking the responsibility. In fact, I enjoyed it and I found that it helped me to switch off from my athletics. It was almost therapeutic.

Over the years I tried various dinner options, including not eating carbohydrates after 7 p.m. It was tough. Because I was the one cooking, I would almost have to cook Charlotte's dinner separately. Then there were the times when we would either go out for dinner or friends would cook for us and I'd be the awkward one at the table, not eating this or that, with people always asking questions.

It was impractical and hard work. I couldn't just make a dish – I had to add in or take out certain ingredients the whole time. I didn't want all those rules and regulations around my food. I started having good carbohydrates with my dinner. It didn't alter my performance or body shape, so I didn't know what all the fuss was about ditching carbs after 7 p.m.

These days I'm not training full time, so on the days I'm doing excercise, I add extra carbohydrates to my meal. If I'm not training, I reduce the amount.

I keep my dinner recipes balanced and easy to make. Time is important during the week and my recipes reflect that. At the weekend, when you have more time, you can get stuck into something a little more involved, like my chermoula lamb dish on page 167.

Meals have to be enjoyable. In many cases, dinnertime is the only time during the day that we get to sit down face to face with our family and loved ones and have a conversation. Charlotte and I always try to sit down at the kitchen table to have our dinner. At first I wanted to eat our dinner in front of the TV, but she got her way. She introduced a ban on phones at the table too. We still stick to it now, and the phone ban has even spread to breakfast. But I'm still cooking the dinner!

CHICKEN, BUTTERNUT SQUASH AND GOAT'S CHEESE LASAGNE

Lasagne was always made on our training camps, everyone living together, gathering around the table and tucking into a fantastic one-pot dish. I've changed it a lot from a normal lasagne by adding chicken and butternut squash, using less white sauce and adding a lot of vegetables. A brilliant dish to make for dinner or as a great get-together meal, and the leftovers go a long way as meals throughout the week.

Preheat the oven to 180°C/350°F/gas mark 4.

Heat a dash of olive oil in a large saucepan over a medium heat. Add the onions and bacon and cook for about 10 minutes, until the onions have softened and are beginning to brown. Add the carrots, celery and garlic and cook for 10–15 minutes, until soft. Stir in the chicken, then stir in the two tins of tomatoes. Fill up one tin with water, then stir that in too. Cover with a lid and simmer for about 1 hour, stirring occasionally, until reduced and thickened.

While the tomato sauce is cooking, roast the butternut squash. Place the squash in a roasting dish. Drizzle with olive oil and season with the dried oregano and some salt and pepper. Cook in the oven for 15–20 minutes, until the squash is soft and brown around the edges. Set aside.

CONTINUED ON PAGE 140

INGREDIENTS

olive oil
2 medium onions, diced
2 rashers streaky smoked bacon, chopped
2 carrots, peeled and chopped
2 celery sticks, chopped
2 garlic cloves, crushed
500g chicken breast fillets, chopped into bite-sized pieces
2 x 400g tins of chopped tomatoes
1 butternut squash, peeled, de-seeded and chopped into 4cm chunks
2 heaped tsp dried oregano
sea salt and pepper
250g spelt pasta lasagne sheets
125g goat's cheese
5 handfuls of spinach leaves, chopped
good bunch of fresh basil leaves

WHITE SAUCE:

1 tsp olive oil
½ small onion, sliced
500ml semi-skimmed milk
1 small bunch of fresh parsley leaves, chopped
pinch of nutmeg
black pepper
35g butter
45g plain flour
70g Parmesan (or your preferred cheese)

SERVES 8

Next make the white sauce. Heat the oil in a medium saucepan over a medium heat. Add the sliced onion and sauté for 5 minutes before adding the milk, parsley, nutmeg and some freshly ground black pepper. Bring to the boil, but watch it carefully because milk will boil quickly. Remove from the heat immediately and strain through a sieve into a bowl or jug.

In a separate saucepan, melt the butter and add in the flour, stirring until it makes a roux. Start adding in the milk one ladle at a time, making sure the milk is thoroughly stirred in before adding the next ladle. Continue until you have a smooth white sauce, then bring it to the boil for a few minutes. Take off the heat and stir in the Parmesan.

Now you're ready to build the lasagne. Place some lasagne sheets on the bottom of a square 25cm x 25cm roasting dish in a single layer, followed by just enough chicken, bacon and veg sauce to cover the sheets. Scatter over some butternut squash, a few spoonfuls of goat's cheese and some spinach. Add another layer of lasagne sheets, followed by the white sauce. Continue making layers in this order until all the ingredients have been used up, making sure to save some white sauce and goat's cheese for the final layer. Sprinkle the basil leaves on top. If you want, you could also break up some small shards of lasagne sheets for extra crunch and scatter them on top.

Cook in the oven for 30 minutes, until the top is golden and the lasagne is bubbling. Allow to stand for 10 minutes before cutting. Serve with a green salad.

CHUNKY CHICKEN AND RED LENTIL STEW

INGREDIENTS

1 tbsp olive oil
1 onion, diced
1 large carrot, peeled and diced
2 large celery sticks, diced
¼ tsp salt
500g chicken breast fillets, diced
200g red lentils
1 litre chicken stock
1 bay leaf
2 tsp curry powder
2 tbsp lemon juice (optional)

SERVES 4

Lentils are relatively quick and easy to prepare. They readily absorb a variety of wonderful flavours from other foods, are high in nutritional value and are available throughout the year. This recipe evolved from another lentil soup I make, but I wanted a little more protein, so I added chicken and let it cook in the lentil broth.

Heat the olive oil in a medium saucepan over a medium heat. Add the onion, carrot, celery and salt and stir to combine. Cover with a lid and let the vegetables sweat for about 5 minutes, until the onion is soft and translucent.

Add the diced chicken, lentils, stock, bay leaf and curry powder. Bring to a boil, then turn the heat down to low and simmer, covered, for 25–30 minutes, until the lentils begin to fall apart and the chicken is cooked through.

Remove the saucepan from the heat and stir in the lemon juice (if using). Add salt to taste. Ladle into bowls and serve.

LEMON AND COCONUT CHICKEN

We all have a repertoire of dishes that seem to be made more often than others, and this dish is definitely in my top five. I use a lot of coconut in my cooking, but in this dish I use creamed coconut, which is the fresh meat of a coconut ground to a semi-solid creamy white paste. It's sold in a hard white block or in easy-to-use sachets, which you simply place in boiling water and then pour into your dish when cooking. It adds so much flavour to a dish and goes really well with lemon and chicken. The portion size given here is per person, so scale up accordingly.

Boil the cubed sweet potatoes until tender, then drain well and keep warm.

Heat the oil in a large frying pan over a medium heat. Sauté the diced onion for 5 minutes, until softened. Add the crushed garlic and cook for 1 minute more, then add the diced chicken and cook for 10 minutes, until lightly browned. Stir in all the chopped vegetables and the green chilli.

Soften the unopened sachet of creamed coconut in a cup of boiling water until it's a thick liquid, then open the sachet and pour the contents into the pan along with the lemon zest and juice. Give everything a stir, and if the creamed coconut is still lumpy and thick, mix in a little water. Stir and simmer for 2 minutes, until the sauce is well combined.

Place the cooked sweet potatoes on a serving plate and cover with the lemon chicken and vegetables. Garnish with the chopped fresh coriander.

INGREDIENTS

100g sweet potato,
peeled and cubed
1 tsp coconut oil
1 small onion, diced
1 garlic clove, crushed
120g chicken, diced
60g courgette, diced
40g asparagus, chopped
1 red pepper, chopped
½ fresh green chilli, deseeded and
finely chopped
1 x 40g sachet creamed coconut
zest and juice of ½ lemon
small handful of fresh coriander,
chopped

SERVES 1

MEXICAN CHICKEN WITH GUACAMOLE, SALSA AND RICE

The only reason you'll eat healthy food again and again is if it's full of flavour. Making your own spice mix is a great way to add flavour to your dishes. This mix goes great with chicken and all the usual Mexican accompaniments. The portion size given here is per person, so scale up accordingly.

To make the spice mix, combine all the spices together in a small bowl. You only need 1 teaspoon of the mix for this recipe, so store the rest in an airtight jar for up to one month.

Melt 1 teaspoon of the coconut oil in a saucepan over a medium heat. Add the chopped onion and cook for 5 minutes, until it starts to brown. Reduce the heat and add the rice, stirring constantly for a further 3 minutes. Add the chopped tomatoes, garlic, chilli (if using), tomato purée and cumin to the rice and turn the heat back up. Stir for 1 minute. Dissolve the stock cube (if using) in the boiling water and then add to the saucepan. Cook for 15–20 minutes, stirring occasionally, until the rice is cooked through.

Melt the remaining teaspoon of coconut oil in a frying pan over a medium heat and add the chicken. Once it has browned, add the pepper and stir in the spice mix. Cook for 10 minutes, until the chicken is cooked through.

Plate up the rice and chicken along with some salad leaves, a dollop of Greek yogurt, guacamole and salsa. Garnish with the coriander leaves and serve.

INGREDIENTS

2 tsp coconut oil
50g onion, chopped
40g basmati rice
80g chopped tinned tomatoes
1 garlic clove, crushed
½ red chilli, deseeded and finely chopped (optional)
1 tbsp tomato purée
¼ tsp ground cumin
200ml boiling water
½ chicken stock cube (optional)
200ml boiling water
100g chicken breast fillet, cut into strips
½ red or green pepper, sliced into strips
1 tsp spice mix (if you like it hot, add a bit more)
salad leaves, such as spinach, rocket and lettuce
60g Greek yogurt
1 tbsp guacamole (page 64)
1 tbsp salsa (page 66)
a few fresh coriander leaves, chopped

MEXICAN SPICE MIX:

2 tbsp chilli powder
2 tbsp paprika
1 tbsp salt
1 tsp onion powder
1 tsp garlic powder
½ tsp cayenne
½ tsp freshly ground black pepper
½ tsp ground cumin

SERVES 1

THAI RED CHICKEN CURRY

INGREDIENTS

4 tbsp Thai red curry paste
1 tbsp extra virgin coconut oil
4 medium chicken breast fillets,
cut into small bite-sized pieces
1 green pepper, diced
1 x 400ml tin of coconut milk
1 tbsp fish sauce
200g quinoa
1 large handful of kale or spinach
1 egg
salt and pepper
juice of 1 lime
2 tbsp Greek yogurt

SERVES 4

I have only recently started to enjoy Thai food after a holiday there, where I sampled the real thing. Although you can't beat a proper Thai takeaway, this curry is easy to make and tastes great. It's definitely worth visiting the Asian markets to get the best ingredients and curry pastes.

Put the curry paste and coconut oil into a large saucepan and fry over a low heat for 2 minutes. Add the chicken and stir to coat evenly with the paste. When the chicken begins to colour and turn white, add the diced pepper and stir for 1 minute.

Pour over the coconut milk and the fish sauce. Bring to a light simmer for about 5 minutes, but don't let it boil as this will curdle the coconut milk.

Meanwhile, half fill the kettle and put it on to boil. Place the quinoa in a separate small saucepan and cover with the boiling water – you want about twice as much water as quinoa by volume. Put a lid on the saucepan and bring to the boil. When it starts boiling hard, turn the heat right down to a minimum and leave to steam. The quinoa is ready when all the water has been absorbed.

Going back to the curry, add the kale or spinach and cook for a further 5 minutes.

CONTINUED OVERLEAF

When the quinoa is cooked, transfer it to a frying pan set over a low heat. Make a well in the middle and crack in the egg. Mix the egg with the quinoa, making sure all the quinoa is covered with egg. Season with salt and pepper and cook for 1–2 minutes while still mixing.

When you're ready to serve, squeeze the lime juice into the curry and add a dollop of Greek yogurt, which will also help with the spice if you're not used to this kind of meal.

To plate up, place the quinoa in the middle of the plate, make a well and spoon the curry into the middle. Add the rest of the Greek yogurt and serve.

QUINOA-ENCRUSTED CHICKEN

INGREDIENTS

50g quinoa
1 egg white, beaten
plain flour, for dusting
40g feta cheese
1 garlic clove, crushed
1 tsp dried Italian herbs
salt and pepper
2 chicken breast fillets

SERVES 2

This is a great summertime recipe if you're having friends around. It's a different take on chicken and the crunch of the quinoa adds a lovely texture.

Half fill the kettle and put it on to boil. Place the quinoa in a small saucepan and cover with the boiling water – you want about twice as much water as quinoa by volume. Put a lid on the saucepan and bring to the boil. When it starts boiling hard, turn the heat right down to a minimum and leave to steam. The quinoa is ready when all the water has been absorbed. Allow to cool.

Preheat the oven to 200°C/400°F/gas mark 6. Line a baking tray with parchment paper.

Place the egg white in a bowl and lightly dust a plate with plain flour. Put the cooked quinoa, crumbled feta, crushed garlic, Italian herbs and a pinch of salt and pepper in a separate bowl and mix well.

Lightly dredge the chicken breasts in the flour. Dip in the egg white, shaking off any excess, then cover with the quinoa. Press the quinoa in firmly to make sure it sticks to the chicken.

Place the coated chicken breasts on the lined baking tray. Cook in the oven for 20–25 minutes, until golden and crispy.

Serve with some red cabbage coleslaw (page 85) for a light summer dish, or for something a little more substantial, try the broccoli and cauliflower gratin on page 88.

CHICKEN, BUTTERNUT SQUASH AND BACON CASSEROLE

INGREDIENTS

5 rashers, cut into large strips
1½ onions, diced
3 large chicken breast fillets, chopped into bite-sized chunks
450g butternut squash, peeled, deseeded and cut into bite-sized chunks
200ml boiling water
1 chicken stock cube
1 x 400g tin of chopped tomatoes
1 tbsp wholegrain mustard
1 tbsp tomato purée
1 tbsp coconut oil
1 tsp dried marjoram
1 tsp dried basil
200g button mushrooms, cut in half
small handful of fresh basil leaves, to garnish

SERVES 4

A slow cooker is perfect for those long winter days when you're out and about, training, working and generally grafting away in the elements. To come home to a warm, comforting dinner that has been simmering away all day is so satisfying. This is a classic casserole and I have included butternut squash for a bit of variety. This is the kind of recipe where you can throw in whatever you want. It also freezes well for future dinners.

Place the bacon and onions in the slow cooker and put the chicken and butternut squash on top. (Tip: To reduce the cooking time by one hour, boil the chopped squash for 8 minutes in a saucepan to soften it before adding to the slow cooker along with the chicken.)

Pour the boiling water into a measuring jug and add the chicken stock cube. Stir until dissolved. In a large bowl, combine the stock with the tomatoes, mustard, tomato purée, coconut oil and herbs. Stir together and pour into the slow cooker.

Cover and cook for 6–7 hours on low or 3–4 hours on high. One hour before the end of the cooking time, add the mushrooms.

Garnish with fresh basil leaves and serve with some steamed broccoli and French beans.

TURKEY BURGERS

Turkey is a great source of protein and eating it regularly can help lower cholesterol levels. I've added mixed seeds to these burgers, which give a great crunch.

Preheat the oven to 200°C/400°F/gas mark 6. Line a baking tray with parchment paper.

Place the sweet potatoes on a baking tray and drizzle with the olive oil. Season with salt and pepper and add the paprika, tossing well so that all the wedges are coated with the oil and seasoning. Cook in the oven for 30–40 minutes, until the edges are brown and crisp.

In a large bowl, combine the minced turkey, diced onion, beaten egg, chopped seeds, Worcestershire sauce and chilli paste. Mix really well – you may need to get your hands in. Once combined, make into four equal-sized patties.

Place the burgers on the lined baking tray and cook in the oven alongside the sweet potatoes for 20–30 minutes, until cooked through. Alternatively, you can pan-fry the burgers.

Serve the burgers with the sweet potato wedges. If you crave the full burger experience, you can serve them in a bread bun. I generally add thinly sliced beetroot and sliced tomatoes in a lettuce leaf 'bun'.

INGREDIENTS

4 sweet potatoes, unpeeled and cut into wedges
2 tsp olive oil
salt and pepper
1 tbsp paprika
500g lean minced turkey
1 small onion, diced
1 egg, beaten
1 tbsp mixed seeds, roughly chopped
2 tsp Worcestershire sauce
1 tsp chilli paste

SERVES 4

TUNA BURGERS

Who said beef burgers are best? Tinned tuna is a common staple in many kitchen cupboards, but finding new ways of using it can be tricky. This recipe is miles away from the usual tuna mayonnaise.

The portion size given here is per person, so scale up accordingly.

Fully drain the tin of tuna, place it in a mixing bowl and break up the meat. Add the beaten egg, diced red onion and Italian herbs. Mix everything together using a fork. Shape into two evenly sized burgers.

Melt the coconut oil in a frying pan over a medium heat. Fry the tuna burgers for 5 minutes on each side, until firm and warmed right through.

Serve alongside the chunky roasted sweet potatoes on page 150.

Serve alongside the chunky roasted sweet potatoes on page 150.

page 150.

INGREDIENTS

1 small tin of tuna (drained weight 130g)
1 medium egg, beaten
1 red onion, diced
1 tsp dried Italian herbs
½ tsp coconut oil

SERVES 1

FISH TAGINE WITH SWEET POTATOES AND ALMONDS

1 tbsp olive oil
1 onion, chopped
good pinch of saffron
600ml hot fish stock or
chicken stock
2 garlic cloves, crushed
3cm piece of fresh ginger, peeled
and grated
½ fresh green chilli, deseeded and
thinly sliced,
plus extra to garnish
1 tbsp tomato purée
2 tsp ground cumin
1 tsp ground coriander
1 tsp ground cinnamon
250g sweet potatoes, peeled and
chopped into small chunks
24 olives, halved
10 cherry tomatoes, halved
1 large carrot, peeled and
thinly sliced
1 tbsp ground almonds
1 tbsp clear honey
zest of 1 orange, juice of ½
700g white fish, cut into
large chunks
small bunch of fresh
coriander, chopped
handful of flaked
almonds, toasted

SERVES 4

I love one-pot dishes. It makes cooking for big groups easier and any leftovers can be used for further meals. Tagines can be healthy, tasty and they're easy to make too – just throw everything into a pot along with the protein of your choice and away you go. The most common tagine is made with lamb, but for variety I'm cooking with white fish, which works just as well.

Heat the oil in a large saucepan over a medium heat. Add the onion and cook for a few minutes, until soft. Meanwhile, put the saffron in the hot stock and let it steep.

Add the garlic, ginger and chilli to the pan and cook for a few minutes more. Add the tomato purée and spices and stir for a few minutes, until fragrant. Add the sweet potatoes, olives, cherry tomatoes, sliced carrot, ground almonds, honey, orange zest and juice and the saffron-scented stock. Simmer, uncovered, for 10 minutes, until the tomatoes have broken down and the sauce has thickened a little.

Add the fish to the pan. Cover and simmer on a low heat for 5 minutes, until the fish is cooked through. Stir in the fresh coriander and toasted almonds.

To serve, scatter over some finely chopped chilli. If it's too spicy, you can add a dollop of natural yogurt to cool it down.

FISH PIE

INGREDIENTS

400g sweet potato, unpeeled and
cut into large chunks
10g butter
pinch of nutmeg
1 large carrot, peeled and grated
1 celery stick, grated
½ courgette, grated
½ fresh red chilli, deseeded and
finely diced
150g Cheddar cheese, grated
2 large ripe tomatoes, chopped
good handful of spinach
large bunch of fresh parsley,
chopped
juice of 1 lemon
250g fish mix, such as hake, ling,
cod and salmon (a supermarket
mix is fine)
salt and pepper
40g feta cheese, crumbled

SERVES 1

I never would have eaten this when I was growing up, as I hated fish. But when I started looking after my diet, I decided to give fish a go again and it didn't disappoint. It's now an integral part of my regime.

Fish pie usually contains a lot of cream and as a result isn't as healthy as you might think. I've tweaked it to add to the nutritional value and get rid of the badness while still keeping it tasty and hearty. I've adapted this recipe from Jamie Oliver. His first book, *The Naked Chef*, really helped me learn how to cook.

Preheat the oven to 200°C/400°F/gas mark 6.

Boil the sweet potatoes in a medium saucepan until tender and cooked through. Drain and put back in the saucepan. Add the butter and a pinch of nutmeg and mash until smooth. Set aside.

Place the carrot, celery, courgette, chilli and grated Cheddar in a circular casserole dish. Scatter over the chopped tomatoes, spinach, parsley and lemon juice. Add the fish and mix all the ingredients well. Season with salt and pepper.

Cover the fish with the mashed sweet potatoes and sprinkle with the crumbled feta cheese. Cook in the oven for 40 minutes, until the sweet potatoes are lightly browned and the fish pie is warmed through.

QUINOA WITH SALMON, ROCKET AND MINT PESTO

You've probably noticed that I use quinoa in a lot of my dishes. This is because it's very high in protein, surprisingly easy to cook and flavour, can be eaten hot or cold and is generally a healthy replacement for potatoes or pasta. It's a versatile grain, but a lot of people don't know how to cook with it. Hopefully this recipe will change that!

To make the mint pesto, mix the peas, Parmesan, garlic, lemon zest, mint leaves (reserve a few for garnish) and olive oil in a pestle and mortar or a blender. Season to taste with salt and pepper and set aside.

Place the quinoa and stock in a saucepan over a medium heat and bring to a boil. Reduce the heat to medium–low and simmer for 15 minutes, until the quinoa is tender and has absorbed all the stock. Remove from the heat, cover and set aside.

Heat the olive oil in a large frying pan over a medium–high heat. Season the salmon and cook for 2–3 minutes on each side, until cooked through. Rest the salmon for 5 minutes and then flake it up.

Transfer the quinoa to a large bowl and combine with three-quarters of the pesto. Stir in the flaked salmon, diced courgette, the rocket and some of the remaining mint leaves. Transfer to a serving bowl, drizzle the remaining pesto over the top and serve.

INGREDIENTS

200g quinoa
125ml vegetable stock
1 tbsp olive oil
4 x 180g skinless salmon fillets
salt and pepper
1 courgette, finely diced
handful of rocket leaves

MINT PESTO:

120g frozen peas, thawed
30g Parmesan, finely grated
2 garlic cloves, crushed
zest of 1 lemon
1 bunch of fresh mint leaves, finely chopped
3 tbsp extra virgin olive oil
pinch of salt and pepper

SERVES 4

SEAFOOD CHOWDER

INGREDIENTS

25g butter
5 celery stalks, diced
2 small onions, diced
2 garlic cloves, crushed
200g cod, skinned and chopped
200ml boiling water
1 fish stock cube
160g prawns
160g mussel meat
270ml double cream
140g Greek yogurt
small handful of fresh parsley
leaves, finely chopped, plus extra
to garnish
4 sprigs of fresh thyme
salt and pepper

SERVES 4

I only started including seafood in my diet a few years ago, so in an attempt to be more adventurous I tried seafood chowder. I loved it! The great thing about a recipe like this is that it's easy to add or remove ingredients, so you can include exactly what you want and it will always be tasty.

Melt half the butter in a large saucepan over a low heat. Add the celery, onions and garlic. Cover the pan and cook for 10 minutes, stirring occasionally, until softened.

Meanwhile, in a separate frying pan, melt the remaining butter on a medium heat. Lightly fry the cod for about 5 minutes, until just cooked.

Pour the boiling water into a measuring jug and add the stock cube, stirring until dissolved.

Add the fish stock to the saucepan of celery and onions along with the fried cod, prawns, mussels, cream, Greek yogurt, herbs and seasoning. Simmer, covered, for 20 minutes, stirring every so often.

Ladle into bowls and serve hot, garnished with a few extra fresh parsley leaves.

PROSCIUTTO-WRAPPED SCALLOPS WITH SAUCE VIERGE

This is the infamous scallops dish from the *Celebrity MasterChef Ireland* semi-final where I burned the first batch and had just enough time to get a second batch on the pan. Prior to *MasterChef* I never ate scallops out of pure ignorance – I simply didn't think I would like them. But when I was preparing for *MasterChef* I said I would try to cook things I wasn't used to in case I was asked to do so on the show, and lo and behold, scallops came a-calling.

First make the sauce vierge. Heat the coriander seeds in a dry pan for about 1 minute, just until fragrant, then crush in a pestle and mortar. Transfer to a bowl and add the remaining sauce vierge ingredients. Stir well and set aside.

Place the scallops in a bowl. Add the olive oil, salt and pepper. Mix to coat the scallops in the oil and seasoning. Wrap a strip of prosciutto around each scallop.

Heat a frying pan over a high heat. Place the scallops in the pan and cook for 1 minute on each side.

Divide the scallops between two plates. Top each scallop with a teaspoon of sauce vierge and serve straight away.

INGREDIENTS

6 scallops
1 tsp olive oil
salt and pepper
6 strips of prosciutto

SAUCE VIERGE:

1 tsp coriander seeds
1 medium tomato, diced
1 garlic clove, crushed
1 tbsp extra virgin olive oil
handful of fresh tarragon leaves, chopped
handful of fresh basil leaves, chopped
juice of ½ lemon

SERVES 2

BAKED SWEET POTATOES STUFFED WITH CHILLI

As you may have gathered, sweet potatoes are a staple in my diet, so it is no surprise that I have switched the potato in this dish to sweet potato. There is nothing like a great-tasting chilli to bring the healthy spud to life.

Preheat the oven to 180°C/350°F/gas mark 4. Line a baking tray with parchment paper.

Slice the sweet potato in half and drizzle with rapeseed oil. Place face down on the lined baking tray and put in the oven. Cook for 45–60 minutes, depending on its size, until cooked through.

Heat a splash of rapeseed oil in a large pan over a medium heat. Sweat the onion for 2–3 minutes, then add the minced beef and season with salt and pepper. Brown the mince, then add the chopped mushrooms, red pepper, courgette and crushed garlic. Stir in the tomato purée, followed by the chopped tomatoes and chilli sauce. Mix thoroughly, making sure the purée has mixed in well. Add a dash of water if it looks too dry – you want the mixture to turn into a sauce. Bring to the boil, then reduce back to a simmer. Add the paprika and a dash of balsamic vinegar and Worcestershire sauce. Mix well and simmer for 20 minutes.

When the sweet potato is cooked, remove it from the oven and scoop out a small amount of potato in order to make a hollow. Fill with mince, then top with crème fraîche and some grated Parmesan.

INGREDIENTS

1 large sweet potato, unpeeled
rapeseed oil
1 medium white onion, diced
300g minced beef
salt and pepper
100g mushrooms, chopped
1 red pepper, chopped
1 courgette, chopped
2 garlic cloves, crushed
1 tbsp tomato purée
1 x 400g tin of chopped tomatoes
2 tsp hot chilli sauce or paste
1 tsp paprika
balsamic vinegar
Worcestershire sauce
1 tbsp crème fraîche
grated Parmesan

SERVES 2

COURGETTE 'SPAGHETTI' BOLOGNESE

Everyone has their own way of making Bolognese. I like mine with a bit of Worcestershire sauce and balsamic vinegar, just like my gran made it. Her secret was to let the sauce simmer for as long as possible. Delish!

To cut down on the calories and because I don't need all that energy in the evening, I replace pasta with courgette ribbons.

Heat the coconut oil in a large pan over a medium heat. Add the onion and garlic and cook for 5 minutes. Add the mince, season with salt and pepper and cook until lightly brown. Mix in the peppers and cook for 3 minutes. Add the chopped tomatoes, tomato purée, Worcestershire sauce and balsamic vinegar and stir well.

Cover the pan and let it simmer for as long as you like. The longer you leave it, the more flavour will be in the dish.

When you're ready to eat, use a vegetable peeler to peel the courgette into strips. Add the strips to the Bolognese and mix for 1 minute to heat through. Serve with a few Parmesan shavings if desired.

INGREDIENTS

1 tsp coconut oil
1 onion, chopped
2 garlic cloves, crushed
300g lean beef mince
salt and pepper
2 red or yellow peppers, chopped
1 x 400g tin of chopped tomatoes
2 tbsp tomato purée
1 tbsp Worcestershire sauce
1 tbsp balsamic vinegar
1 courgette
Parmesan shavings, to serve

SERVES 2

MUM'S STEW

INGREDIENTS

30g plain flour
salt and pepper
500g round or stewing steak,
trimmed and cut into cubes
50g butter
3 carrots, peeled and chopped
2 celery sticks, chopped
1 large onion, diced
1 green pepper, sliced
1 red pepper, sliced
100g mushrooms, chopped
1 x 150g packet Dolmio Stir-In
Roasted Vegetables Pasta Sauce
400ml beef stock
2 tbsp soy sauce
2 tbsp oyster sauce
1 tbsp cornflour, if needed

SERVES 4

Any time I returned home from abroad, this was the dinner Mum would have ready and waiting for me. When I was growing up, Thursday was stew day and it's fair to say it was my favourite day of the week. The sauce was always thick, the meat was always tender and I always wanted more!

Preheat the oven to 220°C/425°F/gas mark 7.

Place the flour in a large bowl with some salt and pepper and mix to combine. Add the cubed steak and coat in the seasoned flour.

Melt the butter in a large frying pan over a medium heat and sauté the meat until brown. Remove the meat with a slotted spoon to a 18cm x 30cm casserole dish.

Lightly sauté the carrots, celery, onion, peppers and mushrooms for 10 minutes, until softened, particularly the carrots. Transfer the vegetables to the casserole dish with the meat.

Add the Dolmio stir-in sauce, beef stock, soy sauce and oyster sauce to the casserole dish. Mix well.

Cover the casserole dish and place in the oven for 30 minutes, then turn down the heat to 160°C/325°F/gas mark 3 and cook for 2 hours more, until the meat is tender. Alternatively, this stew could also be cooked in a slow cooker for 3 hours on a medium heat.

If the stew is too runny, blend 1 tablespoon of cornflour with a drop of water and mix it into the stew. Stir continuously for a few minutes until the stew thickens.

THAI STUFFED PORK OMELETTE

The omelette was the staple meal that I would have after my Saturday morning fartlek session during the winter. It was always so satisfying because I knew when sitting down to eat that I had put in a solid morning's work and I was rewarding my battered body with the right proteins, carbohydrates and fats for it to recover.

Melt 1 teaspoon of coconut oil in a wok set over a medium heat, then add the pork. Once the pork starts to brown, add the tinned tomatoes, red pepper, mushrooms, spring onions, green chilli and 1 tsp of fish sauce. Mix together and cook on a medium heat for 4 minutes, stirring constantly. Add three-quarters of the fresh coriander and cook for 1 minute more.

At this point, either turn the heat down and stir the pork occasionally while you make the omelette or transfer it to a heatproof dish and place it in a warm oven.

Crack the egg and egg white into a small bowl. Add the remaining teaspoon of fish sauce and whisk together.

Melt the remaining teaspoon of coconut oil on a medium heat in a medium frying pan, then add the egg mixture. Tip the pan so that the egg mixture covers the base. Do not stir. Leave for 2 minutes, until the base becomes firm, then transfer under the grill for 2 minutes to cook and lightly brown the top.

As soon as the omelette is cooked, place it in the centre of a plate, spoon in the pork mixture just off centre (it might not all fit), top with the remaining coriander leaves and fold into a parcel. Serve with a green salad or some steamed broccoli and asparagus.

INGREDIENTS

2 tsp coconut oil
120g pork loin steak, cut into strips (no need to cut the fat off)
100g tinned chopped tomatoes
½ red pepper, diced
50g mushrooms, diced
3 spring onions or
1 small onion, chopped
½ fresh green chilli, deseeded and finely chopped
2 tsp Thai fish sauce
good handful of fresh coriander leaves
1 medium free-range egg
1 medium free-range egg white

SERVES 1

CHERMOULA ROASTED LAMB

INGREDIENTS

2kg leg of lamb
saffron and macadamia rice
(overleaf), to serve
Greek yogurt, to serve

CHERMOULA:

2 tbsp cumin seeds
1 tbsp coriander seeds
2 tbsp sweet paprika
2 tsp sea salt
1 tsp ground ginger
1 tsp ground black pepper
2 garlic cloves, peeled
and left whole
1 small fresh red chilli, deseeded
200ml olive oil,
plus extra to drizzle
3 tbsp lemon juice

SERVES 4–6

Chermoula is a Moroccan-inspired marinade for meats. It's amazing what flavours you can muster up by adding herbs and spices together. One of the best presents I ever got was a spice rack. I think chermoula goes best with lamb. The key is to cook the lamb just right, so that it's nice and pink in the middle.

Preheat the oven to 190°C/375°F/gas mark 5.

To make the chermoula, toast the cumin and coriander seeds in a dry pan for 30 seconds, until fragrant. Transfer to a mortar and pestle and crush them with the paprika, sea salt, ground ginger and ground black pepper.

Whizz the garlic, red chilli, olive oil and lemon juice in a blender until smooth, then stir through the spice mixture until well combined.

Place the lamb in a roasting dish. Season with salt and pepper and drizzle with a little more olive oil. Baste the lamb with half of the chermoula and roast for 1 hour. Remove from the oven, baste with the remaining chermoula and cook for a further 30 minutes for medium rare (or longer, depending on how well done you want the meat to be).

Cover the lamb in foil and rest for 20 minutes. Cut into slices and serve with saffron and macadamia rice (overleaf) and Greek yogurt.

SAFFRON AND MACADAMIA RICE

Rice doesn't have to be plain – you can add so many different flavours to get the most out of this grain. The crunch of the macadamia nuts adds a different texture along with the sweetness of the sultanas or currants. This is a great accompaniment to the chermoula roasted lamb on page 167.

Toast the macadamias in a dry frying pan until lightly browned. Remove from the heat and set aside.

Place the stock and saffron in a small saucepan. Bring to a boil, then reduce the heat to low to keep warm.

Heat the oil in a separate large saucepan (one with a lid, as you will need to cover it later) over a medium–low heat. Cook the onion and garlic, stirring, for 3–4 minutes, until softened. Stir in the rice, dried fruit and saffron-scented stock. Season to taste, cover and simmer for 15 minutes.

Remove from the heat and allow to stand, covered, for 15 minutes. You may need to add a little extra water if the rice looks too dry.

Fluff the rice up with a fork. Fold through the toasted nuts, chilli and coriander leaves and serve.

INGREDIENTS

70g macadamia nuts,
roughly chopped
600ml vegetable stock
pinch of saffron
2 tbsp coconut oil
1 onion, diced
3 garlic cloves, crushed
400g basmati or jasmine rice
100g sultanas or currants
salt and pepper
½ red chilli, deseeded
and finely chopped
small handful of fresh coriander,
chopped

SERVES 4-6

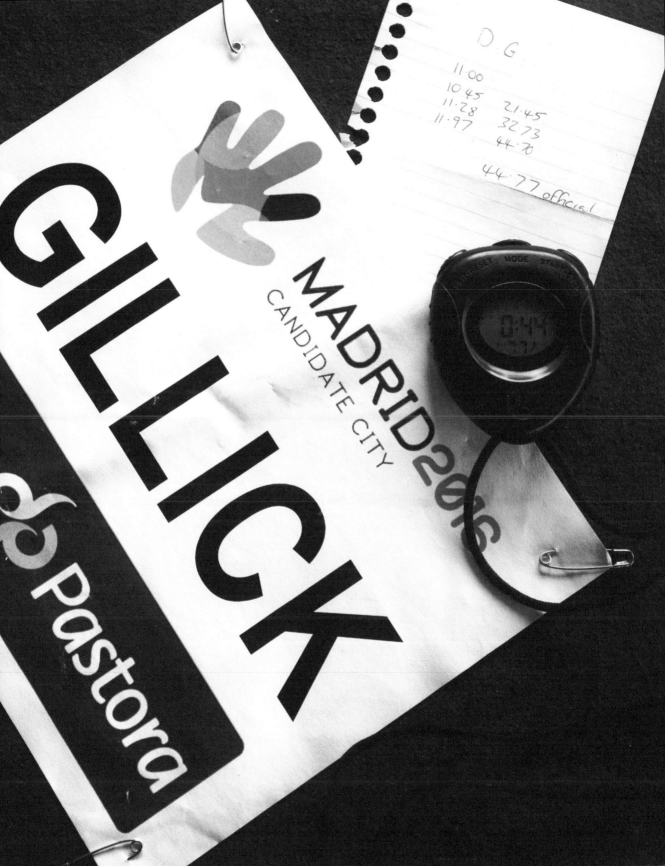

ROASTED BUTTERNUT SQUASH AND CHORIZO RISOTTO

INGREDIENTS

1 small butternut squash, peeled,
deseeded and chopped into
similar-sized chunks
2 tbsp olive or rapeseed oil
salt and pepper
500ml chicken stock
100g chorizo, sliced
1 tbsp coconut oil
1 onion, chopped
2 garlic cloves, crushed
130g Arborio rice (risotto rice)
2 tbsp white wine vinegar
1 tbsp lemon juice
50g grated Parmesan
small handful of fresh
parsley, chopped

SERVES 2

On a cold winter's evening, there is simply nothing like a warm risotto. Risottos usually contain butter and white wine, but I have replaced them with white wine vinegar and lemon juice to keep the flavour. With the oil from the chorizo, it all merges very well. Feel free to add more protein, such as chicken, or give it a boost with extra vegetables.

Preheat the oven to 180°C/350°F/gas mark 4.

Put the chopped squash in a roasting tin and drizzle with the olive or rapeseed oil and a generous pinch of salt and pepper. Cook in the oven for 25 minutes, until tender, cooked through and lightly roasted at the edges. Set aside.

When the butternut squash has about 10 minutes left to roast, heat the chicken stock in a small saucepan.

In a separate large saucepan, lightly sauté the chorizo for a minute or two. Add the coconut oil and let it melt, then add the onion and garlic and sauté for 2 minutes. Add the rice and sauté for another minute or two to coat it in the oil.

Add the white wine vinegar and lemon juice to the pan and stir until it has been absorbed. Then start adding the chicken stock, one ladle at a time. Don't add in another ladle of stock until the previous ladle has been absorbed by the rice. Stir continuously. When all the stock has been absorbed, stir the squash through the risotto. Finally, stir in the Parmesan cheese. Serve garnished with some chopped fresh parsley.

MEXICAN LOADED POTATO SKINS

I eat a lot of sweet potatoes because they release energy slowly, which helps you feel fuller for longer. They tend to be a staple in a lot of athletes' diets and are becoming more popular in kitchens around the country. I'm always looking for different ways to eat and prepare sweet potatoes, so this is my take on the humble loaded potato skin.

Place the chicken in a ziplock bag with the lime juice, chilli flakes and cayenne pepper. Place in the fridge and allow to marinate for at least 1 hour, or overnight if you wish.

Preheat the oven to 180°C/350°F/gas mark 4.

Cut the sweet potato in half and place face down on a lined baking tray. Coat with the melted tablespoon of coconut oil. Bake for 45–60 minutes, depending on the size of the potatoes. The flesh should be soft. If you don't have time to cook the sweet potatoes in the oven, you can microwave them for 10–15 minutes.

While the sweet potato is cooking, melt the remaining teaspoon of coconut oil in a large frying pan over a medium heat. Fry the chicken and the juices from the bag for 10 minutes, until the chicken is cooked through.

Add the sweet peppers, diced onion and jalapeño (if using). Remove the pan from the heat once the chicken is cooked right through.

CONTINUED ON PAGE 174

INGREDIENTS

2 chicken breast fillets, cut into small bite-sized pieces
juice of ½ lime
1 tsp chilli flakes
1 tsp cayenne pepper
1 large sweet potato, unpeeled
1 tbsp coconut oil, melted, + 1 tsp
100g sweet peppers, diced
½ small red onion, diced
1 small jalapeño pepper, de-seeded and finely diced (optional)
50g crumbled feta cheese
2 tbsp Greek yogurt
2 tbsp guacamole (page 64), to serve

SERVES 2

When the potatoes are cooked, scoop out the flesh, leaving a thin layer inside the skin. Place half of the flesh into a bowl (you don't need the remaining flesh for this dish, so keep it in the fridge for another meal). Mash the sweet potato in the bowl and stir in the chicken and pepper mixture.

Refill the sweet potato skins with the mash and scatter the feta cheese on top. Place back in the oven (or under the grill) for 5–10 minutes, until the feta has melted slightly.

Once cooked, top your loaded sweet potato skins with thick Greek yogurt and guacamole. Serve with a fresh side salad.

SPELT PIZZA

SPELT PIZZA BASE:

230g wholemeal spelt flour
2 tsp baking powder
¾ tsp sea salt
2 tbsp olive oil
180ml warm water

SAUCE:

500ml tomato passata
2 garlic cloves, crushed
small handful of fresh
basil leaves, chopped
2 tbsp tomato purée
1 tbsp dried oregano

TOPPINGS:

60g mushrooms, chopped
1 red pepper, diced
50g tinned sweetcorn, drained
50g chorizo, chopped
100g cooked chicken,
chopped into chunks
50g buffalo mozzarella cheese,
chopped into chunks
small handful of fresh spinach
freshly ground black pepper

MAKES 2 PIZZAS

My favourite guilty pleasure has always been pizza. During the summer season, travelling around Europe, I would always treat myself to a pizza if I ran well. I started making my own pizzas when we had friends over, as it can be a great social dish to get stuck into. I experimented with a few bases but I always enjoyed the spelt base the best. It helps that it's a healthier version too. You can buy spelt flour from most supermarkets and health food stores.

Preheat the oven to 220°C/425°F/gas mark 7. Lightly dust a work surface with a little spelt flour.

Mix the spelt flour, baking powder and sea salt together in a large mixing bowl. Make a well in the middle and add the olive oil. Start to mix and add in the water bit by bit until it forms a messy dough. If the dough is getting too wet and sticky, you won't need all the water. Add more flour if it's too sloppy.

Form into a ball, then remove from the bowl and knead for a few minutes on the floured surface. Divide into two.

Use a rolling pin to stretch the base out. Oil your pizza tray or place on an unoiled pizza stone. If you don't have either, use tinfoil. Bake for about 8 minutes on each side, until it just starts to brown. You don't want to fully cook the base now, otherwise it will burn when you cook it with toppings.

CONTINUED ON PAGE 177

Meanwhile, to make the sauce, heat the passata in a saucepan over a medium heat. Add the garlic, basil, tomato purée and oregano and mix well. Bring to the boil, then reduce the heat and allow to simmer and thicken for 5 minutes. Once thickened, set aside and allow to cool.

Once the pizza base has browned, take it out of the oven. Spread with a thin layer of sauce and add your toppings. Put back in the oven until it's cooked to your preference.

BEEF STIR-FRY

This is one of my classic midweek stand-by dishes: quick, easy and versatile. The more colour, the better – feel free to add in or swap with your favourite vegetables. I use either buckwheat or spelt noodles, which are both more nutritious than simple white pasta.

Cook the noodles in boiling water according to the packet instructions. Drain well.

Heat the oil in a large frying pan or wok over a medium–high heat. Add all the vegetables and the garlic and stir-fry for 2 minutes.

Add the beef and 1 tablespoon of the soy sauce and stir-fry for about 5 minutes, until the beef is cooked through.

Add the noodles and remaining tablespoon of soy sauce. Toss to combine until the noodles are heated through.

Transfer to a serving dish and garnish with toasted sesame seeds.

INGREDIENTS

250g buckwheat soba noodles
or spelt noodles
1 tbsp olive oil
1 small head of broccoli,
cut into florets
1 large carrot, peeled
and thinly sliced
½ onion, thinly sliced
½ red pepper, thinly sliced
90g frozen, tinned or fresh
sweetcorn kernels
2 garlic cloves, sliced
300g beef fillet, cut into
thin strips
2 tbsp soy sauce
toasted sesame seeds,
to garnish

SERVES 2

ROAST PORK FILLETS WITH SPICED APPLE SAUCE

Pork isn't a protein I would have eaten a lot of before, but I made a conscious decision to try to add more variety to my meals. Pork is popular in Australia and while down under I picked up this recipe from our local restaurant, Ellacure. Pork and apple are best mates, and by using plenty of herbs and spices you can add loads of flavour to a dish and still keep it healthy. This is a great dish to have with friends and it goes well with the broccoli and cauliflower gratin on page 88.

Place the fennel seeds, sea salt, coriander seeds, peppercorns and cumin seeds in a pestle and mortar and finely grind them all together.

Using a sharp knife, make tiny incisions all over the pork. Drizzle with 1 tablespoon of olive oil and roll in the spice mixture to coat well. Refrigerate for 1 hour or overnight.

Preheat the oven to 160°C/325°F/gas mark 3.

To make the apple sauce, place the apples and onion in a roasting tray, drizzle with the olive oil and scatter over the fennel, star anise, bay leaf and garlic. Bake for 15–20 minutes, until the apples start to soften and the onion is

INGREDIENTS

20g fennel seeds
1½ tbsp sea salt
1 tbsp coriander seeds
1 tbsp black peppercorns
1 tsp cumin seeds
2 x 400–500g pork
tenderloin fillets
2 tbsp olive oil

SPICED APPLE SAUCE:

5 Granny Smith apples, peeled,
cored and cut into wedges
1 onion, cut into wedges
2 tbsp olive oil
1 tsp fennel seeds
4 star anise
1 bay leaf
1 garlic clove, crushed
250ml chicken stock
250ml apple cider
2 tbsp soft light brown sugar
2 tbsp double cream

SERVES 4

slightly caramelised. Before the apples get a tough exterior, pour over half the stock and half the cider. Bake for 15 more minutes, until the apples are tender.

Remove from the oven and transfer the apples to a saucepan, discarding any charred onions. Add the remaining stock and cider and bring to the boil, then reduce the heat to a simmer and cook for 10 minutes, until slightly thickened. Strain through a fine-mesh sieve into a clean saucepan, pushing most of the softened apple pieces and liquid through the sieve. Discard the solids. Add the brown sugar to the pan and a little more stock or water if necessary and blend with a hand blender until smooth. Stir in the cream. Gently reheat the sauce just before serving.

Increase the oven temperature to 180°C/350°F/gas mark 4.

Heat 1 tablespoon of olive oil in a frying pan over a medium–high heat. Add the pork and cook, turning gently, until browned all over. Transfer to a baking tray and cook for 30 minutes, or until cooked through.

Remove from the oven and rest, covered with tinfoil, for 10 minutes. Cut into thick slices. Spoon the sauce onto each plate and arrange the slices of pork on top.

DESSERTS

'AFTER CLIMBING A GREAT HILL, ONE ONLY FINDS THAT THERE ARE MANY MORE HILLS TO CLIMB.'

NELSON MANDELA

I've never been much of a baker; I'm more of a cook. Besides, desserts and treats don't really fit into an athlete's diet. Which is not to say that I didn't enjoy eating them – quite the opposite! My parents love dessert and there is always a homemade tart accompanied by ice cream knocking around the kitchen. On breaks home from training in Loughborough, it was something I certainly stocked up on.

Like anything in life, it's important to have balance, so on the weekends I would allow myself a treat or two. I deserved it.

Nowadays there may be a few more treats, but I try to stick to the same principle about balance.

When I was living and training in America, I started experimenting with making healthier desserts using unusual ingredients. I had a lot more time to myself, so I messed around in the kitchen, trying to come up with various treats. In this chapter you will find some well-known desserts that I have altered with things like stevia and almond flour, and some that are just as they should be. Remember, it's all about balance.

CASHEW NUT BUTTER AND BANANA ICE CREAM

This is a really quick and easy recipe. All you need is frozen bananas on hand and off you go! You don't even need to mess around with an ice cream maker, just a high-powered blender.

Peel and cut the bananas into small chunks and freeze for 1–2 hours, until solid. Once they are frozen, place them in a strong blender with the nut milk and blend until smooth and creamy. This will take a few minutes and you may need to make some periodic pauses and adjustments. Within a few minutes, you should be seeing a thick, creamy mixture in the blender.

Add the cashew nut butter, vanilla extract, cinnamon and a pinch of sea salt. Pulse the blender quickly just to whizz all the ingredients together, and when everything is mixed, serve immediately. Top with additional cashew nut butter and crushed roasted cashews.

INGREDIENTS

3 large, ripe bananas
100ml cashew or almond milk
3 tbsp natural cashew nut butter,
plus extra for topping
¼ tsp vanilla extract
pinch of ground cinnamon
pinch of sea salt
crushed roasted cashews,
for topping

SERVES 2

VANILLA PROTEIN CUPCAKES

INGREDIENTS

80g ground almonds
25g oat flour
25g (1 scoop) vanilla-flavoured
whey protein
1½ tsp baking powder
30g coconut oil, melted
140ml unsweetened almond milk,
at room temperature
4 medium egg whites,
at room temperature
2 tsp vanilla extract

FROSTING:

100g Greek yogurt
15g cocoa powder, sifted
1 tbsp stevia (optional)
1 tsp vanilla extract

MAKES 6 CUPCAKES

Everyone loves dessert and this one is guilt free. Healthy cupcakes with protein and no sugar are becoming more and more popular these days. Protein powder is available in almost every supermarket around the country. I have a high-protein diet and I think it's important for everyone to make sure they are getting enough protein.

Preheat the oven to 180°C/350°F/gas mark 4. If using silicon muffin cases grease all six and place in a muffin tray, if using paper muffin cases simply place them in a muffin tray.

Mix together the ground almonds, oat flour, whey protein and baking powder in a large bowl.

Melt the coconut oil in the microwave, then add to the almond milk, egg whites and vanilla extract in a separate bowl. Whisk or beat for 2–3 minutes to help combine the ingredients. It's important that the egg whites and almond milk are at room temperature because the coconut oil will solidify when mixed with them if they are cold.

Add the wet ingredients to the dry and mix well to form a thick batter.

Evenly distribute the batter between the six greased muffin cases. Bake for 25 minutes until a skewer inserted into the middle of a cupcake comes out clean. Transfer to a wire rack and allow to cool completely. If the cupcakes are still warm, the frosting will melt and drip off.

To make the frosting, mix together the Greek yogurt, cocoa powder, stevia (if using) and vanilla extract in a bowl until well combined. Spread the frosting on top of each cupcake. Eat straight away or store in the fridge.

ALMOND CHOCOLATE CHIP COOKIES

Biscuits have always been my weakness. I love something with a crunch, so much so that I decided to play around with my own recipe. These cookies are easy to make. The problem is stopping yourself eating them all at once!

Preheat the oven to 190°C/375°F/gas mark 5. Line two baking trays with parchment paper.

Place the oil in a small bowl and microwave for about 1 minute, until it has melted.

In a separate large bowl, beat the eggs with the vanilla extract. Add in the ground almonds, stevia, baking powder and a pinch of salt and mix to combine.

Add the melted oil to the cookie dough and mix together. The dough will clump together very quickly. Mix in the chocolate chips.

Drop balls of cookie dough slightly bigger than a tablespoon onto the lined baking trays, spaced well apart to allow them to spread. Bake for 15–20 minutes, until golden. Eat warm or cold.

INGREDIENTS

50g coconut oil
2 medium free-range eggs
1 tsp vanilla extract
300g ground almonds
55g stevia
1 tsp baking powder
pinch of salt
60g dark chocolate, broken into small pieces, or 50g dark chocolate chips

MAKES 12–14 COOKIES

GILLY'S CHOCOLATE CAKE

Who doesn't like chocolate cake? The difference with this recipe is that I came across a new Irish company, Dr. Coy's, that makes amazing nutritional chocolate bars using stevia, a sweetener and sugar substitute extracted from the leaves of the *Stevia rebaudiana* plant, along with 45% Belgian chocolate. The bars are also gluten free and lactose free and come in various flavours. I like to use the chocolate bars to make this cake to add another depth of flavour, but you could also use regular dark chocolate.

Preheat the oven to 150°C/300°F/gas mark 2. Line a 23cm springform tin with parchment paper.

Melt the chocolate and butter in a heatproof bowl set over a pot of simmering water (don't let the bottom of the bowl touch the water). Stir until nearly melted, then take the bowl off the hot water. Stir until completely melted and leave to cool a little.

INGREDIENTS

200g Dr. Coy's chocolate bars or
70% dark chocolate
180g unsalted butter
8 eggs, at room temperature
150g + 15g stevia
200g ground almonds
60g cocoa powder, plus
extra to decorate
1 vanilla pod, split in half lengthways and the seeds scraped out
pinch of salt

MAKES ABOUT 8 SLICES

In a large bowl, beat two whole eggs, six egg yolks (put the whites in a separate spotlessly clean, dry bowl) and 150g of stevia very well. Add the ground almonds, cocoa powder and vanilla seeds and fold in until combined. Finally, fold in the melted chocolate mixture until combined.

Beat the egg whites until frothy. Add a pinch of salt and continue to beat until soft peaks form. Add the remaining 15g of stevia and beat again until stiff peaks form. Gently fold the egg whites into the chocolate mixture, stirring as little as possible to keep all the air in.

Pour the batter into the lined tin and bake in the oven for 30 minutes. The cake should be cooked on top but still quite wobbly. Transfer to a wire rack to cool completely, then cover with cling film and chill in the fridge overnight.

The next day, release the sides of the springform tin and transfer the cake to a serving plate. Dust with a little extra cocoa powder to decorate.

COCONUT CHIFFON CAKE

250g unsalted butter, softened
and diced, plus extra for greasing
450g caster sugar
4 eggs
450g self-raising flour, sifted
250ml coconut milk
2 tsp vanilla extract

FILLING:

300g sour cream
210g caster sugar
60ml milk

FROSTING:

225g icing sugar, sifted
2 egg whites
1 tbsp glucose syrup
1 tsp cream of tartar
1½ tsp vanilla extract
210g desiccated coconut

SERVES 10-12

When planning our wedding, Charlotte and I decided to ask a few close family and friends to make a cake for our dessert table. We wanted to have an array of cakes as opposed to just one. Of course, if we were asking people to make one, I had to bake one myself too, so this is the cake I made. With all the stress in the days leading up to our wedding, I also had to make a cake. I thought baking was meant to be relaxing! We got there in the end, though, and had a table of six cakes, including my 93-year-old gran's fruit cake, which is the cake we cut for the paps – sorry, I mean photographer.

I picked up this recipe from my housemate Lyndsay while living in Australia. She loved to bake and taught me so much. Everyone needs a housemate like her!

Preheat the oven to 170°C/340°F/gas mark 3. Grease and line the base and sides of two 22cm loose-bottomed cake tins (if you don't have two tins, you can cook the cakes in two batches).

Beat the butter and 450g of caster sugar with an electric beater until it turns lighter in colour and creamy. Add the eggs one at a time, beating well after each addition.

Add the flour, coconut milk and vanilla extract and fold in with a metal spoon until well combined.

CONTINUED OVERLEAF

Divide the batter evenly between the prepared tins and bake for 25–30 minutes, until golden and a skewer inserted into the centre comes out clean. Cool the cakes in the tins for 10 minutes, then turn out onto a wire rack to cool completely.

To make the filling, place the sour cream, caster sugar and milk in a bowl and stir to combine.

Carefully slice each cake in half horizontally. Place one cake layer on a serving plate and spread with half of the filling. Top with the other half of the cake. Repeat with the second cake. Alternately you can layer the two cakes on top of one another, splitting the filling in three.

For the frosting, place the icing sugar, egg whites, glucose syrup and cream of tartar in a heatproof bowl set over a pan of simmering water. Whisk for 3–4 minutes, until thick and doubled in volume. Transfer to an electric mixer, then add the vanilla and whisk on high speed for 5 minutes, until it is very thick and has increased in volume.

Using a palette knife, spread the frosting over the top and sides of the cake to cover it completely. Press the coconut into the frosting.

RASPBERRY AND ROSE MERINGUE TART

500g fresh or frozen raspberries
(thawed and drained well
if frozen)
2 tsp rosewater (optional)
40g arrowroot
80ml cold water
2 tbsp lemon juice
260g caster sugar
4 eggs, separated
50g unsalted butter

**SWEET
SHORTCRUST
PASTRY:**

180g plain flour, sifted
2 tbsp icing sugar, sifted
pinch of salt
125g unsalted butter,
chilled and diced
1 egg yolk
60ml ice water

SERVES 6

Before I started *Celebrity MasterChef Ireland*, I was really worried about pastry. I'd never made it before and wasn't looking forward to the challenge. Prior to the show I played around with this recipe. It was tricky at first, but once you master this pastry you can make any filling you want. As it was summer, I opted for raspberries and it went down very well! To make life a little easier, you can always use ready-to-roll shop-bought pastry.

First make the sweet shortcrust pastry. Place the flour, icing sugar and a pinch of salt in a food processor and pulse to combine. Add the butter and whizz until it looks like fine crumbs. Alternatively, mix the flour, icing sugar and salt together in bowl and use your fingertips to rub in the butter to form fine crumbs.

Add the egg yolk and ice water and pulse again just until it comes together in a smooth ball. Wrap the dough in cling film and chill in the fridge for 30 minutes.

Preheat the oven to 180°C/350°F/gas mark 4.

Lightly dust a board with flour, then roll out the pastry to a 5mm thickness. Lift the pastry into individual 10cm loose-bottomed tart tins or one 23cm loose-bottomed tart tin and gently press into the base and up the sides to line it, trimming the excess pastry. Line with baking paper and fill with baking weights or uncooked rice.

CONTINUED OVERLEAF

Bake for 10 minutes, then remove the paper and weights and return to the oven for a further 3–5 minutes, until pale golden and dry. Allow to cool on a wire rack while you make the filling.

Purée the raspberries in a blender, then pass through a fine sieve into a saucepan, pressing down with the back of a spoon to extract as much juice as possible (this may take 10 minutes to do). Discard the solids left in the sieve and stir in the rosewater (if using).

Place the arrowroot and cold water in a small bowl and stir to combine. Add to the raspberry purée along with the lemon juice and 85g of the caster sugar. Place the saucepan over a low heat and cook, stirring, for 3–4 minutes, until thick.

Add the egg yolks one at a time, beating well after each addition, then add the butter and stir until melted. Remove from the heat and allow to cool, then chill in the fridge for 30 minutes. Once it has cooled, fill the tart shell with the chilled raspberry mixture.

Meanwhile, put the egg whites in a spotlessly clean, dry bowl. Whisk with an electric beater until soft peaks form, then gradually add the remaining caster sugar, beating until stiff peaks form. Transfer the meringue to a piping bag fitted with a star-shaped 0.5cm nozzle.

Pipe the meringue decoratively over the tart, then brown briefly under a hot grill or with a kitchen blowtorch.

ROASTED PEARS

INGREDIENTS

4 ripe pears, unpeeled
100g ricotta cheese
½ tsp ground cinnamon
4 tbsp clear honey
8 amaretti biscuits, crushed

SERVES 4

Roasted pears are brilliant as a dessert. Soft and really moist, they go well with something cool and crunchy. To keep it on the healthy side, use ricotta instead of ice cream, but a few amaretti biscuits won't hurt anyone.

Preheat the oven to 190°C/375°F/gas mark 5. Line a baking tray with parchment paper.

Cut each pear in half, then use a small spoon to scoop out the core and make a hollow in the centre of each half. Place on the lined baking tray, cut side up.

Dollop 1 tablespoon of ricotta cheese into each hollow. Sprinkle with the cinnamon and drizzle with a little honey.

Roast the pears for 10 minutes, then remove from the oven and cover with the amaretti biscuit crumbs. Return to the oven for another 10 minutes, until the pears are golden brown.

STRAWBERRY, RICOTTA AND WHITE CHOCOLATE TART

We are all entitled to a dessert now and again, and as part of training week I would have a treat meal on a Saturday or any time I felt I deserved something sweet. I also made this for the dessert task on *Celebrity MasterChef Ireland* and it's fair to say the lads enjoyed it!

Place all the biscuits in a large ziplock bag and seal it tightly, then crush the biscuits by bashing them with a rolling pin (or you could use a food processor). Transfer to a bowl and mix well with the melted butter. Press into the sides and base of a 25cm loose-bottomed tart tin, then press down with the back of a spoon to smooth it out. Chill in the fridge for 30 minutes.

To make the filling, beat the ricotta and 115g of icing sugar until smooth, then fold in the orange juice, the chopped white chocolate and half the chopped pistachios. Spoon into the chilled tart base, then put back in the fridge and chill for 4 hours.

Half an hour before serving, mix the strawberries with the remaining tablespoon of icing sugar and the orange zest. Transfer the tart to a serving platter, then pile on the strawberries. Top with the grated white chocolate and the remaining chopped pistachios.

INGREDIENTS

100g amaretti biscuits or biscotti
100g digestive biscuits
100g unsalted butter, melted and cooled
500g fresh ricotta cheese
115g icing sugar +
1 tbsp icing sugar
zest and juice of ½ orange
80g white chocolate, half finely chopped, half grated
60g shelled pistachios, chopped
400g fresh strawberries, hulled and halved

SERVES 8–10

YOGURT SPARKLERS

INGREDIENTS

200g fresh blueberries
300g Greek yogurt
1 tbsp honey

MAKES 5-6 ICE POPS

When I was a kid growing up in Dublin, 10p went a long way. You could buy a tenpenny bag, a giant cola bottle or the best: a sparkler ice pop! Life was full of tough decisions back then. This is my simple, healthy take on an ice pop. It uses Greek yogurt as its base with fruit stirred through it. It's easy to add your favourite fruit or a combination of a few different ones, so play around with the recipe.

Blend half the blueberries in a food processor. Slice the remaining berries in half and place a few in each ice pop mould.

Combine the yogurt, honey and the blended berries in a small bowl. Use a fork to stir through the berry purée.

Pour the mixture into the moulds. Insert the ice pop sticks and transfer to a freezer for at least 3 hours, until solid.

CHERRY BERRY CRUMBLE

You can't beat a crumble for a hearty dessert. I have changed a few things in my recipe. For starters, I use a variety of berries for an antioxidant boost. I also use a natural sweetener called stevia instead of sugar and I've replaced plain white flour with almond flour, which adds a little extra flavour. Lots of change for the better, but I can guarantee you will go back for more!

Preheat the oven to 190°C/375°F/gas mark 5.

Combine the blueberries, raspberries, cherries, almond flour, lemon juice and stevia in a medium bowl. Spoon the berries into a square 25cm x 25cm baking dish.

For the topping, mix together the almond flour, oats, cinnamon and stevia, then rub in the butter with your fingertips until the mixture resembles breadcrumbs.

Scatter the topping evenly over the fruit. Bake for 30 minutes, until bubbly.

INGREDIENTS

200g fresh or frozen blueberries
(thawed and drained
well if frozen)
200g fresh or frozen raspberries
(thawed and drained well if
frozen)
200g fresh cherries, stones and
stalks removed
1 tbsp almond flour
1 tbsp fresh lemon juice
1 tbsp stevia

TOPPING:

80g almond flour
50g porridge oats
¾ tsp ground cinnamon
½ tsp stevia
70g butter, chilled and diced

SERVES 8

SWEET POTATO BROWNIES

Charlotte is the one who smuggles chocolate into our house, but I'll be honest – I eat it too. I came home one day to find Charlotte working away on a healthier version of brownies using sweet potatoes. It sounded odd to me, but I was pleasantly surprised with the outcome. They were delicious!

Preheat the oven to 180°C/350°F/gas mark 4. Line a square 25cm x 25cm baking tray with parchment paper.

Combine the eggs, grated sweet potato, melted coconut oil, honey and vanilla extract in a large mixing bowl and stir together until they are well mixed.

Add the cacao powder, baking powder and baking soda and stir. Finally, fold in the coconut flour until just combined. Don't be tempted to add more coconut flour, as it will absorb too much moisture, which will result in dry brownies.

Pour the batter into the lined baking tray and cook for 25–30 minutes, until a skewer inserted into the centre comes out clean and dry. Cool on a wire rack for 5–10 minutes before carefully removing the brownies from the tin.

To serve, cut into squares and dust with a little cacao powder. Or you could melt some dark chocolate and drizzle it over the top. Serve with fresh fruit and a dollop of Greek yogurt.

INGREDIENTS

2 eggs, beaten
1 medium sweet potato, peeled and grated
120ml melted coconut oil
115ml honey
2 tsp vanilla extract
40g raw cacao powder, sifted, plus extra for dusting
1 tsp baking powder
1 tsp baking soda
2½ tbsp coconut flour

MAKES 12 BROWNIES

INDEX